IRISH ANCESTORS

ALSO AVAILABLE

Louis Bell
POPULAR IRISH POETRY

Laurence Flanagan
IRISH PROVERBS

Padraic O'Farrell
ANCIENT IRISH LEGENDS
IRISH FOLK CURES
IRISH CUSTOMS
IRISH FAIRY TALES
IRISH SAINTS
IRISH SURNAMES

Dáithí Ó hÓgáin
IRISH SUPERSTITIONS

Diarmaid Ó Muirithe
A GLOSSARY OF IRISH SLANG
AND UNCONVENTIONAL
LANGUAGE
IRISH WORDS & PHRASES

IRISH ANCESTORS

JOHN GRENHAM

Gill & Macmillan

Gill & Macmillan Ltd
Hume Avenue, Park West
Dublin 12
with associated companies throughout the world
www.gillmacmillan.ie

0 7171 3628 0

Original text design by
Identikit Design Consultants, Dublin
Print origination by Carole Lynch
Printed and bound by Nørhaven Paperback A/S, Denmark

This book is typeset in 10/15 pt Adobe Garamond.

The paper used in this book comes from the wood pulp of managed forests. For every tree felled, at least one tree is planted, thereby renewing natural resources.

A CIP catalogue record for this book is available from the British Library.

1 3 5 4 2

CONTENTS

ONE

INTRODUCTION

WHY BOTHER?

'What are you interested in that lot for? Sure aren't they all dead?'

My mother was not one of nature's genealogists, but she was squarely in a long Irish tradition. For all the brouhaha about genealogy, in medieval and early modern Irish society the real concern was kinship, not ancestry. The Irish were never ancestor-worshippers. The purpose of the family tree was to demonstrate whom you were related to, and there was no compunction about pruning the tree or grafting on to it to produce the right sort of relations. As far as I know my mother didn't invent second cousins, but she did spend endless hours with my aunts patiently teasing out every acquaintance's every possible family relationship. When I asked the central question of genealogy, the four year old's 'where did I come from', the answer was simply 'here.' And until quite recently, that was the answer for the vast majority of Irish people whether they were Southern Catholic or Northern Presbyterian.

Things have changed. Families are smaller and more scattered. Growing up, I had more than seventy first cousins, almost all within a fifty mile radius of my home. My son, by comparison, has three first cousins 150 miles away. When tribes shrink and scatter like this, the question of origins becomes more insistent and the answer more problematic. Why prosperity should have this effect is open to debate, but prosperity also provides the time and the education to explore the question. Only with the economic growth of the last two decades have people within Ireland begun to search out their own forebears and to develop and respect the records that make that search possible.

In any case genealogy has at least one intrinsic redeeming value. The more you come face to face with the irreducible variety of the past, the less seriously you take received notions of race, class and religion. No notion of racial purity can survive the day-to-day erosion inflicted by the sheer diversity that emerges as you follow families through generation after generation. The fact is that everyone's ancestry is mixed. We are all mongrels, and nowhere more than here on these islands.

BEFORE YOU START

There are a few persistent myths about Irish genealogy:

- **The records were all destroyed in 1922.** Wrong. The Public Record Office in Dublin was indeed destroyed in 1922 along with virtually all its contents. Where genealogy is concerned the most significant losses were the nineteenth-century census returns, the Church of Ireland parish registers and the testamentary collections. Anything not in the PRO — non-Church of Ireland parish records, civil records of births, marriages and deaths, property records and later censuses, to name only a few — survived, and for much of the material that was lost, there are abstracts, transcripts and fragments of the originals.

- **Irish research is impossibly difficult.**
  Wrong. Actually there is quite a compact set of relevant records, almost all held centrally in Dublin or Belfast. If you start with enough information — in particular a place of origin in Ireland — research is really quite straightforward.
- **All the records for Northern Ireland are held in Belfast and those for the Republic of Ireland are in Dublin.**
  Wrong again. Until 1922 the entire island was one administrative unit. Both Dublin and Belfast repositories have at least copies of the pre-1922 records, with those in Belfast largely but not completely confined to the nine historic counties of Ulster. Only after 1922 are the records different.

- **There are seventy million Americans with some Irish ancestry. There must be a fortune to be made.**
  No there isn't.

WHAT DO YOU NEED TO KNOW?

Location, location, location — and location — and as much else as possible. Unless your ancestor had an outlandish surname, the minimum you'll need to know is the county of origin, and if the surname is common, even a county or a parish may not be specific enough. The vast majority of Irish records before the 1860s are location-specific, and reliance on fragments or local census substitutes resulting from the 1922 disaster means that even neighbouring parishes may have quite different record profiles. Both standard guides to Irish research, my own *Tracing Your Irish Ancestors* (Gill & Macmillan, 2nd edition, 1999) and James Ryan's *Irish Records* (Flyleaf Press, 2nd edition, 1998), include detailed listings by county showing what records survive.

The basic principles of research on Irish ancestors are the same as those for any research:

- **Be logical**. Start from what you know and use it to find what you don't know. Do not presume that you must be connected to the

O'Kellys of Uí Máine and try to stretch their seventeenth-century pedigree to fit into your family. Start from Grandpa Joe Kelly and work back.

- **Be sceptical**. Genealogy is not forensic science — nobody (one hopes) is going to jail because of what you uncover — but a mistaken assumption can cause endless frustration and wasted effort.
- **Be patient**. Researching your family history is the work of months and years. Computers and the Internet notwithstanding, there are very few shortcuts.
- **Be cunning.** Your poor great-granny's rich second cousin may have left a lot more in the way of family records than your poor great-granny herself. Following these may tell you a lot more than looking for direct evidence.

TALK TO YOUR GRANNY

Start with your family, the ones still alive. Many families have at least one hoarder of information, someone who makes it their business to collect and record the doings of the relatives and who is only too glad to have someone to sit and talk about it all. Without running an interrogation, you need to be systematic about writing down (or even taping) what you hear. It is not too important at this stage to be certain about everything, but even a half-remembered fact could provide a vital clue at a later stage. Apart from anything else, you will get a much better sense of the people than that provided by bare records of names and dates.

Family papers if they exist are also an obvious starting point, and you should take 'papers' quite literally. For genealogy, virtually anything can supply evidence — photographs, family Bibles, letters (and postmarks), mass cards, newspaper cuttings, deeds, cancelled cheques — and you should take a note, or preferably a copy, of anything which could possibly be relevant.

I KNOW IT'S IN HERE SOMEWHERE

Covering even a few generations of any family can very rapidly yield a few hundred individuals, each with their own events and documentation. Add the fact that most researchers put down and pick up family history intermittently, sometimes with intervals of years, and you have a recipe for much frustration and head scratching. For some brave and well-organised souls, a few stout notebooks and a shoebox of index cards are perfectly adequate. For most though, a dedicated genealogy program can save time and aggravation.

There are hundreds of programs designed which allow you to store, link, print, publish on the Internet, and more. All of them are relatively inexpensive and some are shareware, allowing you to try them out before you pay. The better-known shareware programs are Brother's Keeper, Cumberland Family Tree, and Family Scrapbook. The most popular commercial programs are Personal Ancestral File, Reunion, Family Tree Maker, the Master Genealogist, and Ultimate Family Tree. All these are North American and the best way to investigate them is online. Go to a search engine such as Google and enter the program name. You can find a comparison of their features at **www.lkessler.com/gplinks.shtml.**

One word of caution. Some of the programs have 'luxury' or 'gold' editions that will include umpteen CDs of genealogical data as well as the program. Almost all this data is North American and will therefore be useless to someone researching ancestors in Ireland.

You have two parents, four grandparents, eight great-grandparents, sixteen great-great-grandparents and so on. So, presuming a conservative three generations per century, thirty generations ago, around the year A.D. 1000, you should have had 1,073,741,824 ancestors — more than a billion. This is several times the population of the planet in A.D. 1000. What is the explanation? It's simple. The calculation assumes that none of the couples over those thirty generations was in any way related. If you marry your first cousin, your children will only have six great-grandparents, not eight; twelve great-great-grandparents, not sixteen; and so on. At a stroke you will have removed more than 600 million of those notional ancestors a thousand years ago, and that's still presuming none of the other generations were related. In fact the chances are that almost all your ancestors were related to each other in some way. In settled rural societies everyone was at least a fourth or fifth cousin. The fact is, we're all more related than we realise. As you walk down a Dublin street every stranger you see has many ancestors in common with you, however far back it may be.

WHAT WILL YOU FIND?

That depends. What you know determines what you will find out. For most people, those researching Catholic tenant farmers, the earliest limit for research is usually the starting date of the local Catholic parish records, which varies widely from place to place. It would be unusual for the records of such a family to go back much earlier than the 1820s. There are many exceptions, though, with local censuses or tenants' lists for particular areas, early directories for towns, some very good records for smaller denominations and, inevitably, copious records for those who had property of any description. The single biggest obstacle to extending research to the extent possible for families born in many other countries is the collapse of native Gaelic culture in the mid-seventeenth century, which left an almost unbridgeable gulf of five or six generations, even for the Gaelic aristocracy.

RESEARCH SERVICES

If distance, lethargy or frustration strikes, it may be a good idea to commission research. There are two main ways of doing this in Ireland. First you can pay an individual to carry out research for you. The usual process is to outline (briefly) what you already know in a letter. If research is feasible, the genealogist will then quote you a rate for a specified number of hours' work, with an explanation of the records to be covered. Payment is normally in advance. You should keep in mind that you are paying for time and expertise, not results: it is, after all, possible that the genealogist will find nothing. The Association of Professional Genealogists in Ireland acts as a regulating body to maintain standards among its members. You can obtain a membership list at **indigo.ie/~apgi.**

The other route is via the network of local heritage centres. You will find a full list in Chapter 9. If you know your ancestor's county but not a specific location, these centres, with their databases of church records in particular, are the most practical route. Some of the best centres also have database copies of many of the other sources. The usual procedure is for the centre to carry out a preliminary, relatively inexpensive, search to confirm that they do indeed have relevant records before quoting you for a full search.

The National Archives of Ireland and the National Library of Ireland both have a genealogy service for personal callers, in which an experienced researcher will examine whatever information you have and outline the best course of research. This service is free.

STARTING RESEARCH QUESTIONNAIRE

Was your ancestor born, or married, or did he or she die in Ireland after 1863?

If the answer is yes, do you know their precise location in Ireland?

And if you know the location, was your ancestor in Ireland in 1901?

If you know the location and your ancestor or any members of his or her family were living in Ireland in 1901, the 1901 and 1911 census returns are probably the best place to start. With the information here, it should be relatively simple to identify relevant entries in the state records of births, marriages and deaths — marriage entries are most useful. From here, all the records relating to occupation and to the locality are available, including church records.

If you know only the county, it may be an idea to commission a heritage centre to search its database if it has completed computerising church records for the county (see Chapter 9).

If you don't know if your ancestor was in Ireland in 1901, you can start either with state records of births, marriages and deaths (Chapter 2), or with church records (Chapter 4). State records are easier to use and probably more accessible. Marriage records are particularly useful. Church records are generally more comprehensive.

If you don't know a precise location, but your ancestor recorded a birth, death or marriage in Ireland after 1863, you should start with state records of births, marriages and deaths (Chapter 2). The relevant entry in these records will give you a precise location. With this you will then be able to use the 1901 and 1911 census returns (Chapter 3), the relevant church records (Chapter 4), and all the records relating to the locality.

If you cannot find a relevant entry in state records — all too possible — what you do next depends on the circumstances:

- If you know a death took place in Ireland, the post-1858 Calendars of Wills and Administrations might give you a location.
- If you know your ancestor's occupation in Ireland, occupational sources might supply a location (Chapter 7).
- If you have a precise date of emigration, particularly towards the end of the nineteenth century, passenger and immigration lists might supply a location of origin.
- If you know none of these, you can check surname distribution in Ireland to give you some idea of where in Ireland the surname was most common and start work on the records for this area (Chapter 5). However the chances of success are very slim.
- If your ancestor emigrated, it is probably more advisable to work on the records in the country of immigration.

If your ancestor was not born, did not die, or get married in Ireland after 1863, were any of your ancestor's brothers and sisters or other relations born, or did they get married, or die in Ireland after 1863?

If the answer is yes, you should concentrate for the moment on locating these people in the records. The location information you uncover will lead you to your ancestor (see page 20).

If the answer is no, was your ancestor (or any of his or her siblings) a non-Roman Catholic who married in Ireland after 1844?

If yes, all marriages except those between Catholics are registered from 1845. If you can identify the relevant entry, it will provide details of the preceding generation as well as a location and occupation (Chapter 2). From here local church records, occupational records and records relating to the locality are available.

If no, do you know a precise location in Ireland?

If the answer is yes, local church records are the best direct source of family information. To identify the relevant church or parish, you first need to know the civil parish. You can find this from the Townlands Index (Chapter 5). The civil parish is also necessary to use land records and other records relating to locality. It may also be an idea to commission a heritage centre to search its database, if it has completed computerising church records for the county.

If you know the county, you will still have to identify the precise area, generally a townland or civil parish.

If you have some idea of the placename but don't know where it is in the county, check the Townlands Index. If the surname is unusual enough, you may be able to narrow down the potentially relevant areas using a count of householders or the Index of Surnames. You could also use the full name index to Griffith's Valuation (Chapter 5).

If your ancestor lived in Ireland before the nineteenth century, then:

- If he or she was a member of the property-owning classes, there is a good chance you will find something in records of wills, the Registry of Deeds, the Genealogical Office or in newspapers.
- If he or she was not a member of the property-owning classes, check local county source lists, especially for estate records, census substitutes and gravestone inscriptions. However you are crossing the boundary between genealogy and local history and your chances of finding information are not good.

Your ancestor was not born, did not marry, and did not die in Ireland after 1863 and you don't know where in Ireland he or she came from.

You will have to find a location. How you do this depends on what else you know:

- If you have some idea of the placename but cannot locate it in Ireland, check the Townlands Index.

- If all you know is the name of the individual, then (unless the surname is very unusual) you will have to find the location of origin in some other way.
- If you also know the surname of your ancestor's spouse or other relatives, it may be possible to narrow down the areas in which both surnames occur in the early nineteenth century using count of householders or the Index of Surnames or the Griffith's CD index. Again, this depends on how common the surnames were.
- If your ancestor had an occupation in Ireland other than tenant farmer, trade directories and occupational records might provide a location.
- If you know when your ancestor emigrated and where to, passenger and immigration lists and material on the Irish abroad may provide at least a county of origin.

TWO

THE GENERAL REGISTER OFFICE

ACCESS

The natural place to begin a search for your ancestors is with the state registration of births, deaths and marriages and, theoretically at least, the system is straightforward. All births, deaths and marriages have been registered in Ireland since 1864, while non-Roman Catholic marriage registration began nineteen years earlier in 1845. The system is very similar to those used in England and Wales, and in Scotland, where registration began in 1838 and 1845 respectively.

In essence, the birth, death or marriage was (and is) recorded locally and periodically forwarded to a central collating body, the General Register Office (GRO), to make copies and indexes. The original registration was then returned to the local authority. The geographical areas used for registration were based on the old Poor Law Unions, which were also used as the basis for the nineteenth-century public health system. This is the reason the GRO in the Republic of Ireland is still administered by the Department of Health. The Northern Ireland GRO is now part of the

Northern Ireland Statistics and Research Agency. The GRO in Dublin has copies and master indexes for all of Ireland from 1845 to 1864 for non-Catholic marriages, from 1864 to 1922 for all births, marriages and deaths, and for the twenty-six counties from 1922. The Belfast office has copies and indexes of births and deaths for areas now in Northern Ireland from 1864. Northern Ireland marriage records from 1845 to 1922 are held in the District Registrar Offices. In both jurisdictions the GRO is the only part of the system officially open for public research.

Anyone looking at records more than sixty or seventy years old needs to be aware of the possibility of variant surname spellings. In Irish records variant spellings are a certainty. Before the twentieth century the O and Mc prefixes were treated by record keepers as entirely optional. McCarthy may appear as Carthy, Carty, Cartie; O'Brien will usually be Brien (or Brian, Bryan or Bryen). In addition, you should keep in mind that the vast majority of the population were illiterate or semi-literate, very often spoke Irish as their first language and invariably had more pressing concerns than the precise spelling of their surname. From the seventeenth century on Irish surnames were translated, pseudo-translated, transcribed phonetically and transposed to their nearest English equivalent. So *Mac Gabhainn*, from *gabhann*, meaning 'blacksmith', became Smith, Gowan or McGowan; *Ó hEarrachtáin* became Harrington; *Mac an Dheanaigh*, from *deánach*, meaning 'dean', became McAnany (or McEnany, McEneny or McAneany) phonetically, or Deane by translation, or even Bird because of a spurious resemblance to *eán*, the Irish for bird. These absurdities were mirrored by the Irish education system in the twentieth century, with its insistence that everyone had two surnames, the original Irish with an *Ó* or a *Mac*, and a lesser English version which was, naturally, the one in everyday use. Where surnames were awkward enough not to have an Irish original, one had to be made up. Even at the age of eight it seemed odd that my father and myself had different Irish surnames. Given this, it is not unusual for members of the same Irish family to appear in the same record with different surnames.

The registration system may be straightforward, but using it for research is anything but. In the Dublin GRO the research room is cramped and overcrowded, in summer especially, and the arrangements for viewing both the indexes and the extracts from the registers are so cumbersome that it can take several hours to carry out a simple piece of research that should take no more than a few minutes. The upshot, perhaps indeed the intended result, is that experienced researchers will go out of their way to avoid having to use it. In Belfast the research arrangements are more sensible, but it is necessary to make an appointment a few weeks in advance. There are some workarounds which are outlined below.

As already noted, under the original system the local registrars forwarded their records to Dublin where they were copied and then returned to the local office. As well as the master indexes for the entire country, the General Register Offices also contain microfilms of all these copy registers. In Dublin the indexes are available to the public on the first floor of 8 Lombard Street at a fee of €1.90 per five years searched, or €15.24 for a general search. A general search consists of daylong (six hours) access to either the birth or death indexes, or six days of access to the marriage indexes. *Only the indexes are open to the public*; to obtain the full information contained in the original register entry it is necessary to purchase a printout from the microfilm at €1.90 per entry. These printouts are supplied for information only and have no legal standing. Full certificates, for use in obtaining passports or in testamentary transactions, cost €6.98.

In Belfast a general search of records assisted by members of the GRO staff for any period of years and any number of entries costs st£19 per hour, while an index search 'with limited verification of entries by staff' costs st£8 for six hours or part thereof. A full certificate costs st£9.

OTHER MEANS OF ACCESS

It is also possible to carry out research on some GRO records in other ways:

- The registrar's offices around the country sometimes allow access, although this is at the discretion of the local officials. At times, particularly for surnames that are very common in a specific area, this can be the only way to reconstruct a whole family, since the research is on the original registers rather than indexes (see Chapter 9).
- Some of the local heritage centres, including Clare, Derry, Mayo and Tipperary South, now have database transcripts of these local registers. Only commissioned research is possible.
- Some transcripts of the records have been made available on the Internet. For example Waterford death records up to 1900 are now searchable online (see Chapter 8).
- The Family History Library of the Church of Jesus Christ of Latter-Day Saints, the

Mormons, has microfilm copies of much of the GRO holdings as follows:

- Indexes (births, marriages and deaths) 1845/1864 to 1958
- Birth registers 1864 to March 1881 and 1900 to 1913
- Marriage registers 1845 to 1870
- Death registers 1864 to 1870.

These records can be accessed via the family history centre attached to every Mormon temple.

- The second edition of the *British Isles Vital Records Index* CD-ROM, produced by the Mormons, includes detailed abstracts from Irish birth records from 1864 to 1875 inclusive.

INFORMATION GIVEN

Whatever way you approach the records, the information they contain remains the same, and it is a good idea to know how they came into being. One of the peculiarities of registration is that, although the local registrars were responsible for the registers themselves, the legal obligation to register births, deaths and marriages actually rested with the public and was enforced with hefty fines. To avoid these, parents would sometimes amend a child's official birth date to ensure it fell within the required twenty-one days.

Births

From a research point of view only the following information is of interest:

- the child's name
- the date of birth
- the place of birth
- the name, surname and dwelling place of the father
- the name, surname and dwelling place of the mother, and occasionally
- the name, residence and qualification of the informant.

Although it was not obligatory to register a first name for the child, the very small proportion for which no first names were supplied appear in the index as, for example 'Kelly (male)' or 'Murphy (female)'.

Birth entries can be difficult to identify correctly from the indexes without precise information about date and place. Even with such information the high concentrations of people of the same surname within certain localities can make it difficult to be sure that a particular birth registration is the relevant one.

A general word of warning about civil registration. A certain proportion of all three categories simply went unregistered. The thoroughness of local registration and the safety of the registers depended very much on local conditions and on the individuals responsible. Frustrated experience in cross-checking from other sources such as parish and census records suggests that as much as ten to fifteen per cent of marriages and births simply do not appear in the registers.

Marriages

Useful information includes:

- the parish in which the marriage took place
- the names, ages, residences and occupations of the persons marrying
- the names and occupations of their fathers, and occasionally
- the names of the witnesses

Marriage entries are the most useful of the records, both because they provide fathers' names, thus giving a direct link to the preceding generation, and because they are the easiest to identify from the indexes.

Deaths

Information consists of:

- the place of death
- the age at death, and occasionally
- the name, residence and qualification of the informant.

Unlike death records in many other countries, Irish death records are not very useful for genealogical purposes; there was no obligation to record family information, and the 'age at death' is often very imprecise. This much said, these records can sometimes be of value. The 'person present at death' was often a family member and the relationship is sometimes specified in the register entry. Even the age recorded may be useful since it at least gives an idea of how old the person was thought to be by family or neighbours.

RESEARCH IN THE INDEXES

From 1864 to 1877 the indexes consist of a single yearly volume in each category — births, marriages and deaths — covering the entire country and recording all names in a straightforward alphabetical arrangement. The same system also applies to non-Catholic marriages registered from 1845. From 1878 the yearly volume is divided into four quarters, each quarter covering three months and indexed separately. So a search for a name in the 1877 births index means looking in one place in the index, while in the 1878 index you have to check four different places, each of the four quarters. From 1903, in the case of births only, the indexes once again cover the entire year and only from this year do they also supply the mother's maiden surname. Each index entry gives the surname, first name, registration district, volume and page number. The deaths indexes also give the reported age at death. The 'volume and page number' simply make the reference for the original register entry, which you will need in order to obtain the full information, either on microfilm or with a photocopy.

TIPS

Surname

The order followed in the indexes is strictly alphabetical, but it is absolutely necessary to keep possible variants of the surname in mind. The best advice is to list as many variants as possible before you begin. Otherwise you may find yourself having to re-order and search the same volumes more than once, a prospect to be avoided at all costs.

> A large measure of scepticism is necessary with regard to dates of births, marriages and deaths reported by family members before 1900. This is especially true for births; the ages given in census returns, for example, are usually inaccurate, and appear to have been given in round figures such as fifty, sixty and seventy. These should be treated with particular

caution. The true date of birth is usually well before the one reported, sometimes by as much as fifteen years. Strange as it may seem to us now, with our birthday parties and horoscopes, it would appear that very few people actually knew their precise date of birth. Perhaps they had more pressing things on their minds. Moreover since, after middle age at least, no one feels as old as they actually are, a guess usually produces an underestimate. Whatever the explanation, it is always wiser to search a range of the indexes before the reported date, rather than after.

First name

Among the vast majority of the population the range of first names in use in the nineteenth century was severely limited. The anglicisation of the earlier Gaelic names was highly restrictive and unimaginative: John, Patrick, Michael, Mary and Bridget occur with almost unbelievable frequency in all parts of the country. Combined with the intensely local nature of surnames, reflecting the earlier tribal areas of the country, this can present serious difficulties when using the indexes. For example a single quarter of 1881, from January to March, might contain twenty or more Patrick (Mc)Carthy (or Carty) registrations, all in the same registration district of Co. Cork. A further obstacle is the fact that it is very rare for more than one first name to be registered. Thus someone known to the family as Patrick Joseph (Mc)Carthy will almost certainly appear in the index as simply Patrick. Of course you could examine all the original register entries, but unless some other piece of information such as the parents' names or the townland address can be used to cross-check, you will almost certainly not be able to identify which, if any, of the original register entries is the relevant one. The persistent imprecision regarding ages and dates of birth makes things even more complicated. Over the seven or eight year period when the relevant birth could have taken place, there might be fifty or sixty births of the same name in the one county. One way around this, if the precise district is known, is to examine the original registers themselves to build a picture of all the families in which the relevant name occurs. As already mentioned, the originals are still kept in the local registrars' offices.

Registration district

Because of the original arrangements for administering the system, registration districts were and still are largely identical with the old Poor Law Unions. Since these were based on natural catchment areas normally consisting of a large market town and its rural hinterland, rather than on the already existing administrative divisions of townland, parish and county, registration districts for births, marriages and deaths cut right across these earlier boundaries, a fact which can be very significant for research. Thus, for example, Waterford registration district centred in the town of Waterford also takes in a large part of rural south Co. Kilkenny. The only comprehensive guide as to which towns and townlands are contained in each registration district is to be found in a series of pamphlets produced in the nineteenth century by the Registrar-General's Office for the use of each local registrar. These are collected as *Townlands in Poor-law Unions* (ed. G. A. Handran, 1997, Higginson, Salem Ma.), copies of which can be found in the National Library (reference: Ir. 9141 b 35) or in the reading room of the National Archives. To go in the other direction, to find out what registration district a particular town or townland is in, the standard source is the *Alphabetical Index to the Towns, Townlands and Parishes of Ireland*. Three editions of this were published, based on the census returns for 1851, 1871 and 1901. In the first two the registration district is recorded as the Poor Law Union; in the 1901 Index it does not appear in the body of the work but is added in an appendix. Copies of these can be found on open access in the National Library, the National Archives, the General

Register Office itself or in any library. If the original townland or address of the family being researched is known and the search narrowed to a single registration district, then at least some of the problems in picking out the relevant entry, in the births indexes particularly, can be significantly reduced.

RESEARCH TECHNIQUES

Births

You should approach the birth indexes with as much information as possible from other sources. If the birth took place between 1864 and 1880, the family was Catholic and the relevant area is known, you might be better off trying to identify a baptism from parish records first. In many cases, if you simply want the information rather than a certificate, the parish record itself will be enough. If you know the area but not the date, the 1901 and 1911 census returns might give you at least an approximate age and year of birth. If you know the names of other members of the family and the order of their birth but not the area and date, you might have to search a wide range of years in the indexes, noting all births of the names which occur in the family, and then try to work out which births of the relevant names occur in the right order in the same registration district.

Marriages

As long as you are careful with surname variants and you know the names of both parties, research in the marriage indexes is straightforward. If two people married each other, then obviously the registration district, volume and page number references for them in the indexes have to be the same. You simply need to cross-check the two names in the indexes, working back from the approximate date of birth of the eldest child, if you know this, until you find two entries in which all three references correspond. The 1911 census records the number of years a couple have been married, obviously very useful in tracking the marriage entry.

Deaths

Again it is essential to uncover as much information as possible from other sources before starting a search of the death indexes.

- If you know a date of birth from parish or other records, the 'age at death' given in the index along with the registration district provides at least a rough guide as to whether or not the death recorded is the relevant one.
- If you know the location of a family farm, the approximate date of death can often be worked out from the changes in occupier recorded in the Valuation Books of the Land Valuation Office (see Chapter 5).

- If the family had property, the Will Calendars of the National Archives after 1858 can be the easiest way to pinpoint the precise date of death.
- Along with the names of the fathers of the parties marrying, the marriage register entries sometimes also specify that one or both of the fathers is deceased, which may at least provide an end point for any search for his death entry.

LIVING RELATIVES

It is very difficult to use the records of the General Register Office to trace the descendants, rather than the forebears of a particular family. The birth indexes after 1902 record the mother's maiden name as well as the name and surname of the child, so it may be possible to trace all the births of a particular family from that date forward. Uncovering the subsequent marriages of those children without knowing the names of their spouses is a much more difficult proposition, however.

THREE

CENSUS RECORDS

After General Register Office records, the natural source to turn to is Irish census returns. The good news is that full government censuses were taken every ten years between 1821 and 1911. The bad news is that almost all the nineteenth-century returns were destroyed, either by official order or by the 1922 fire in the Public Record Office. The earliest full censuses for the entire island date from 1901 and 1911. Because of this (a small bit of good news) the normal rule that the original returns remain closed for a century was suspended in the 1970s and microfilm copies of both 1901 and 1911 are available at the National Archives of Ireland. Only 1901 for Northern Ireland is available at the Public Record Office of Northern Ireland. The 1901 microfilm has also long been held by the Family History Library of the Church of Jesus Christ of Latter-Day Saints, the Mormons, and can be ordered through the Family History Library attached to any LDS temple. Portions of the 1901 returns for particular areas of Ireland are also online (see Chapter 11) or published (see my own *Tracing Your Irish Ancestors*, 1999, 2nd ed., or James G. Ryan's *Irish Records,* 1998, 2nd ed.). In addition, significant fragments of the earlier censuses have survived for some parts of the country (see below for details).

1901 AND 1911 RESEARCH

The basic problem is finding the right set of returns. Ideally you should know the relevant street or townland. In both 1901 and 1911 the returns were collected by the District Electoral Division (DED), a subdivision of the county used for electoral purposes. For rural areas, if you identify the placename in the 1901 Townlands Index, this will also give you the name and number of the DED in which the townland is situated. County-by-county volumes on open shelves in the National Archives reading room go through the DEDs in numerical order for both 1901 and 1911, giving the name and number of each of the townlands they contain. To order the returns for a specific townland in the National Archives, you need to supply the name of the county, the number of the DED and the number of the townland, as given in these volumes. For the cities of Belfast, Cork, Dublin and Limerick separate street indexes are available on open shelves in the reading room. Again each street or part of a street is numbered, and these numbers are necessary to order specific returns. Between 1901 and 1911 some changes took place in the District Electoral Divisions and their numbering is different in some cases. There is no separate townlands index for 1911, but the changes are minor so that a DED numbered 100 in 1901 may be 103 in 1911 and can be found simply by checking the divisions above and below 100 in the 1911 volume for the county.

INFORMATION GIVEN

The 1901 and 1911 returns record:

- name
- relationship to the head of the household
- religion
- literacy
- occupation
- age
- marital status
- county of birth
- ability to speak English or Irish
- number of years married (1911, women only).

The returns also give details of the houses, indicating the number of rooms, outhouses and windows, and the type of roof. Members of the family not present when the census was taken are not recorded.

TIPS

Age

This most obviously useful piece of information is also one that needs to be treated with the most scepticism. Very few of the ages given in the two sets of returns actually match precisely. In the decade between the two censuses most people appear to have aged significantly more than ten years.

Location

When you know the names of all or most of the family, as well as the general area, it is possible to search all the returns for that area to identify the relevant family and thus pinpoint them. This can be particularly useful when the surname is very common; the likelihood of two families of Reillys with precisely the same children's names in the same area is remote.

Cross-checking

At times, again when a name is common, it can be impossible to identify from information uncovered in civil or parish records a particular family as the one you are searching for. In such cases, when you know details of the subsequent history of the family — dates of death or emigration, or siblings' names for instance — a check of the 1901 or 1911 census for the family can provide useful circumstantial evidence.

Marriages

The requirement in the 1911 census for married women to supply the number of years of marriage is obviously a useful aid when subsequently searching civil records for a marriage entry. Even in 1901 the age of the eldest child recorded can give a rough guide to the latest date at which a marriage is likely to have taken place.

Living relatives

Children recorded in 1901 and 1911 are the parents or grandparents of people now alive. The ages — generally much more accurate than those given for older members of the family — can be useful in trying to uncover later marriages in civil records. When used together with Land Valuation Office records (see Chapter 5) or the voters' lists of the National Archives, they can provide an accurate picture of the passing of property from one generation to another. Luckily the Irish attitude to land means that it is quite unusual for rural property to pass out of a family altogether.

NINETEENTH-CENTURY CENSUS FRAGMENTS

1821. Only a few volumes survive for parts of Cos Cavan, Fermanagh, Galway, Meath and Offaly (King's County). These are now in the National Archives. They record:

- the name
- the age

- the occupation
- the relationship to the head of the household
- the acreage of the landholding
- the number of storeys the house has.

1831. Most of the remaining fragments relate to Co. Derry. Information on the house was dropped and religion added.

1841. Literacy, date of marriage and 'family members who died since 1831' were added. Only the returns for the parish of Killeshandra in Co. Cavan survive. The 1841 and 1851 census returns were sometimes used as proof of age when state old-age pensions were introduced in the early twentieth century, and the forms detailing the results of searches in the original returns to establish age have survived and are found in the National Archives for areas in the Republic of Ireland, and the Public Record Office of Northern Ireland for areas now in its jurisdiction.

1851. Most of the surviving returns relate to parishes in Co. Antrim.

1861, 1871, 1881 and 1891. The official destruction of the returns for these years was lamentably thorough. Virtually nothing survives. The only transcripts are contained in the Catholic parish registers of Enniscorthy (1861) and Drumcondra & Loughbraclen, Co. Meath (1871).

CENSUS SUBSTITUTES

Almost anything recording more than a single name can be called a census substitute, at least for genealogical purposes. What follows is a listing, chronological where possible, of the principal substitutes. For details of the parishes they cover, you should see my own *Tracing Your Irish Ancestors* (1999, 2nd ed.) or James G. Ryan's *Irish Records* (1998, 2nd ed.).

Eighteenth and nineteenth centuries

- *1703–1838. The Convert Rolls* (ed. Eileen O'Byrne, Irish Manuscripts Commission, 1981) lists those converting from Catholicism to the Church of Ireland.
- *1740.* Names of Protestant householders for parts of Cos Antrim, Armagh, Derry, Donegal and Tyrone.
- *1749.* The Elphin diocesan census, which is arranged by townland and parish, lists householders, their religion, the numbers, sex and religion of their children, and the numbers, sex and religion of their servants.
- *1766.* This is a somewhat ham-fisted attempt at a census carried out by Church of Ireland

rectors on the instructions of the government. Many of the returns give only numerical totals. All the original returns were lost in 1922, but transcripts survive for some areas and are deposited with various institutions. The only full listing of all surviving transcripts and abstracts is in the National Archives reading room on the open shelves.

- *1796.* Spinning-Wheel Premium Entitlement Lists are a record of those entitled to a government subsidy to the weaving trade covering almost 60,000 individuals, which show only the name of the individual and the civil parish in which he lived. A microfiche and CD-ROM index to the lists are available.
- *1824–38.* Tithe Applotment Books (see Chapter 5).
- *1847–64.* Griffith's Valuation (see Chapter 5).
- *1876. Landowners in Ireland: Return of owners of land of one acre and upwards ...* (London: Her Majesty's Stationery Office, 1876), reissued by the Genealogical Publishing Company, Baltimore, 1988, gives the names, addresses and acreage of 32,614 owners of land in Ireland in 1876. Only a minority of the population actually owned the land they occupied.

Various dates

Freeholders. From the early eighteenth century freeholders' lists were drawn up regularly, usually because of the right to vote which went with freehold of property over a certain value. This was of interest for only a small minority of the population.

Voters' lists and poll books. Voters' lists cover a wider range of population than freeholders' lists since they also include freemen of the various corporations. Poll books are the records of votes actually cast in elections.

Electoral records. No complete collection of the electoral lists used in the elections of the twentieth century exists. The largest single collection of surviving electoral registers is to be found in the National Archives, but even here the coverage of many areas is quite skimpy.

Valuations. Local valuations and revaluations of property were carried out with increasing frequency from the end of the eighteenth century, usually for electoral reasons. The best of these record all householders.

FOUR

CHURCH RECORDS

Church records are by far the most useful of Irish genealogical sources. They can give a complete overview of a family and sometimes even several generations of multiple families. Because of the destruction of census returns in 1922 and the relatively late start of state registration of births, deaths and marriages, for most families church records are the only direct evidence of their ancestry in the early nineteenth century.

ROMAN CATHOLIC RECORDS

Parishes

The Catholic parish system is largely a product of the eighteenth and nineteenth centuries. Official repression of Roman Catholicism in the eighteenth century was a mixed blessing. Whatever its effect on individual clergymen, it forced a degree of flexibility in Church organisation which allowed parishes to change and expand to cater for shifting population patterns. As a result Catholic parishes tend to be larger and more populous than those of other denominations, with records that are extensive and time-consuming to search. Equally, the names of Catholic parishes can be difficult to pin down, since they may incorporate parts of earlier parishes or take the name of the major town. Westport parish in Co. Mayo for example, has also been known as Aughaval, Oughavall, Lecanvey and Drummin. As in so many other areas of Irish genealogy, you may need patience and some lateral thinking to pinpoint the parish you want.

Because parish records are the single most important Irish record source, you should keep some points in mind:

- Searching microfilm copies of the original registers, particularly Roman Catholic registers, can be mind-numbingly tedious. Researchers can wake up from a trance in front of a microfilm reader several years further on in the records from their last episode of self-awareness, but with no memory of searching the intervening years, and may have to go back and re-check. Unless you have the powers of concentration of a Zen master you will need to take frequent breaks and keep a written note of the precise period searched.
- For the same reason it is almost unthinkable to search the records of every parish in a county by hand. If this is what you're facing, you should consider narrowing the search to the marriage

registers, which are much less extensive, or commissioning a search from the local heritage centre if they have a database transcript — unless, of course, you know what the sound of one hand clapping is.

- Be very sceptical of reported ages. If another source has informed you that a baptism should be recorded in 1850, the minimum you should be prepared to search is 1847 to 1852. And the maximum? Anything up to fifteen year discrepancies can happen.
- Anyone who has spent time on the microfilms will embrace an index or transcript with joy and relief. But be wary. The original registers already contain mistakes made by the all too human clergy, and a transcript always adds another layer of error from the even more human transcriber. This is especially true of material on the Internet. If you don't find something in a transcript, you cannot presume there isn't something in the original. If you do find something, you should check it against the original anyway.

Dates

The earliest Catholic parish records in the country appear to be the fragments for Waterford and

Galway cities, dating from the 1680s, and for Wexford town, dating from 1671. Generally speaking early records tend to come from the more prosperous and anglicised areas, in particular the towns and cities of the eastern half of the island. In the poorest, most densely populated rural parishes of the West and North, precisely those that saw most emigration, the registers very often do not begin until the mid or late nineteenth century. However the majority of Catholic registers begin in the first decades of the nineteenth century, and even in poor areas, if a local tradition of Gaelic scholarship survived, records were often kept from an earlier date. Killenaule in rural Tipperary has records from 1742.

What Catholic records contain

Catholic registers consist mostly of baptismal and marriage records. For some reason, possibly because the clergy were already overworked, the keeping of burial records was much less thorough than in the Church of Ireland. Fewer than half the parishes in the country have a register of burials before 1900, and even where they do exist, the registers are generally intermittent and patchy. Strangely, given the cultural importance of funerals, almost no Catholic burial registers exist for the southern half of the island.

Baptisms and marriages are recorded in either Latin or English, never in Irish. Parishes in the richer areas where English was more common tended to use English, while in Irish-speaking parishes Latin was used, but there is no absolute consistency. The Latin presents very few problems since only first names were translated, not surnames or placenames, and the English equivalents are usually self-evident. The only possible difficulties are: *Carolus* (Charles); *Demetrius* (Jeremiah, Jerome, Darby, Dermot); *Eugenius* (Owen or Eugene); *Gulielmus* (William); *Honoria* (Hannah, Nora); *Ioannes* or *Joannes* (John); and *Jacobus* (James). The only other Latin needing explanation is that used in recording marriage dispensations.

Baptisms. Most baptismal registers record:

- date of baptism (not birth)
- child's Christian name
- father's name
- mother's maiden name
- address, usually a townland, of the parents
- names of the sponsors or godparents.

A full Latin entry might read:

> *Baptisavi Carolum, filium legitimum Ioannii Carthy et Honoriae Sullivan de Kilquin. Sponsoribus, Danielus Quirk, Johanna Donoghue.*

More often the entry is abbreviated to:

> *Bapt. Carolum, f. l. Ioannii Carthy et Honoriae Sullivan, Kilquin.*
> *Sp: Danielus Quirk, Johanna Donoghue.*

Which translates as: 'I baptised John, legitimate son of John Carthy and Nora Sullivan of Kilquin, with godparents Daniel Quirk and Johanna Donoghue.' In many cases even the abbreviations are omitted and the entries simply record dates, names and places.

Marriages. Marriage registers always give:

- the date
- the names of the persons marrying, and
- the names of the witnesses.

Other information that may be supplied includes the residences (of all four people), ages, occupations and fathers' names. In some rare cases the relationships of the witnesses to the people marrying are also specified. A typical Latin entry would read:

> *In matrimonium coniunxi sunt Cornelium Buckley et Margaritam Hennessy, de Ballybang. Testimonii: Danielus McCarthy, Brigida Kelliher.*
>
> Abbreviated, the entry reads:
>
> *Mat. con. Cornelium Buckley, Margaritam Hennessy, Ballybang.*
> *Test. Danielus McCarthy, Brigida Kelliher.*

This translates as Cornelius Buckley and Margaret Hennessy, of Ballybang, are joined in matrimony; witnesses, Daniel McCarthy, Brigid Kelliher.

> Because of the expansion of Roman Catholic parishes over the course of the nineteenth century, the apparent starting dates of many Catholic registers can be deceptive. Obviously if a parish was created in 1850, its records only begin in 1850. But the areas in the new parish did not just pop into existence; they were previously in another parish which almost certainly has records from before 1850. For example the Catholic parish of Abbeyleix in Co. Laois (Queen's County) has records listed in the National Library catalogue as starting in 1824. In fact the parish was only created in that year. Before then its records will be found in Ballinakill which has records from 1794. So where surviving records appear too late to be of interest, you should always check the surrounding parishes for earlier registers.

Where are Catholic records?

- The National Library has microfilm copies of registers from about ninety-six per cent of Catholic parishes from all thirty-two counties of Ireland. All are available for public research, with the exception of parishes in the dioceses of Kerry, and Cashel and Emly. For Kerry you need permission from the bishop, but this is usually faxed to the National Library after a phone call. No records from the diocese of Cashel and

Emly are available for research. The local Archbishop withdrew permission for public research in the 1980s, with the aim of obliging researchers to use the services of Tipperary Family History Research (see Chapter 9).

- A separate microfilming project was carried out by the Public Record Office of Northern Ireland for the six counties under its jurisdiction. The results are generally identical to the National Library copies, although in some cases PRONI has used a later cut-off date.
- The Church of Jesus Christ of Latter-Day Saints also has an extensive collection of Catholic parish register microfilms made up partly of copies of some of the National Library films and partly of material microfilmed by the Church itself. Of the 1,153 parishes in the country the LDS library has records of 398.
- The Irish Genealogical Project has computerised almost all Irish parish records, though there remain some significant gaps. The records are held in local heritage centres throughout the country and not directly accessible to the public. You have to commission research. Details of the centres will be found in Chapter 9.
- For published works and the Internet, see Chapter 8.

Researching Catholic records

If you know the parish. Simple. The National Library microfilm catalogue is organised by diocese, the PRONI catalogue alphabetically, and the LDS catalogue by subject and geographical area. All these catalogues are now online. For the LDS it may take several weeks for a family history centre to order and receive the film. Be careful of variant parish names.

If you know a placename but not the parish. Any of the Townland Indexes from 1851, 1871 or 1901 will show the relevant civil parish. The 1851 index is searchable online at **www.seanruad.com** or **www.ireland.com/ancestor**. There are then a number of ways to find the corresponding Catholic parish. Lewis's *Topographical Dictionary of Ireland* (1837) is the only nineteenth-century source that systematically relates civil to Catholic parishes. Although sometimes vague, it is the basis of all the other sources that show the link between civil and Catholic parishes. These include Brian Mitchell's *Guide to Irish Parish Records* (Genealogical Publishing Co., Baltimore, 1987), the National Library 'Index of Surnames' (or 'Householders' Index') and James Ryan's *Irish Records* (Flyleaf Press, 1998).

If you know the county but not a placename. This is where things start to get interesting. It is most emphatically not a good idea to lash into all the records in a county one by one. That way lieth madness and despair. To undertake a general search of a county, you have to narrow your focus first. You can do this by using the count of householders in the National Library 'Index of Surnames' which is based on the Primary Valuation of 1847–68 (see Chapter 5), or via **www.ireland.com/ancestor** which does a similar count. It helps if the surname is unusual or if you know more than one surname. Be vigilant for variant spellings. Or of course you could pay for a search of the parish records from the local heritage centre if they have the records.

If you don't even know the county. Then you'll have to find it somehow (see Chapter 8).

CHURCH OF IRELAND RECORDS

Parishes

In general the Church of Ireland retained the older medieval parochial divisions in use before the Reformation, which were also used for administrative purposes by the secular authorities. So civil parishes, which were the basic geographical units in early censuses, tax records and land surveys, are almost identical to Church of Ireland parishes. The records of each parish cover a relatively small area and are fairly easy to search in detail — that is, where they have survived the destruction of 1922.

After the Church of Ireland ceased to be the Established Church in 1869 its marriage records before 1845 and its baptismal and burial records before 1870 became the property of the state and therefore public records. Unless the local clergyman was in a position to demonstrate that he could house these records safely, he was required to deposit them in the Public Record Office. By 1922 the original registers of nearly a thousand parishes, more than half the total for the country, were stored at the Public Record Office. These were all destroyed in the fire at the PRO on 28 June of that year. Fortunately a large number of registers had not found their way into the PRO. In many cases local rectors had made a transcript before surrendering the originals, and local historians and genealogists using the PRO before 1922 had also amassed collections of extracts from the registers.

Dates

Church of Ireland records are generally much older than those of the Roman Catholic Church. From as early as 1634 local parishes were required to keep records of christenings and burials in registers supplied by the Church authorities. As a result a significant number, especially of urban parishes, have registers dating from the mid-seventeenth century. The majority however start in the years between 1770 and 1820; the only countrywide listing of all Church of Ireland parish records which gives full details of dates is the National Archives catalogue, a copy of which is also to be found at the National Library. In addition the Irish Family History Society has published *A Table of Church of Ireland Parochial Records* (ed. Noel Reid, IFHS, 4th ed., 2001), and the *Guide to Church Records: Public Record Office of Northern Ireland* (PRONI, 1994) gives details of PRONI's holdings.

What Church of Ireland records contain

Burials. Unlike their Catholic counterparts, the majority of Church of Ireland clergymen recorded burials as well as baptisms and marriages. The burial registers can also be of interest for other denominations; the dead are apparently quite ecumenical. Information given is rarely more than:

- the name
- the age, and
- the townland.

Clear family connections can be difficult to establish from these.

Baptisms. Most Church of Ireland baptismal records supply:

- the child's name
- the father's name
- the mother's Christian name, and
- the name of the officiating clergyman.

Quite often the address is also recorded. The omission of the mother's maiden name can be an obstacle to further research. From about 1820 the father's occupation is supplied in many cases.

Marriages. Since the Church of Ireland was the Established Church, the only legally valid marriages, in theory at least, were those carried out by an Anglican clergyman. In practice, of course, recognition was given to marriages of other denominations. None the less the legal position of the Church of Ireland meant that many marriages of members of other Protestant Churches are recorded in Church of Ireland registers. The registers do not give a great deal of information, usually only:

- the names of the parties marrying, and
- the name of the officiating clergyman.

Even addresses are not common, unless one of the parties is from another parish. More comprehensive information is to be found in records of marriage banns, where these exist. Although it was obligatory for notification of the intention to marry to be given in church on three consecutive Sundays, written records of these are relatively rare. After 1845, when non-Catholic marriages were registered by the state, the marriage registers record all the information contained in state records including occupations, addresses and fathers' names.

Marriage licence bonds. As an alternative to marriage banns, members of the Church of Ireland could take out a marriage licence bond. The parties lodged a sum of money with the diocese to indemnify the Church against there being an obstacle to the marriage; in effect the system allowed the better off to purchase privacy. The original bonds were all destroyed in 1922, but the indexes are available at the National Archives. The Dublin diocesan index was published as part of the *Index to Dublin Will and Grant Books*, RDKPRI 26, 1895 (1270–1800) and RDKPRI 30, 1899 (1800–1858). The Genealogical Office holds abstracts of prerogative marriage licence bonds from 1630 to 1858 (GO 605–7), as well as marriages recorded in prerogative wills (GO 255–6).

Other. As well as straightforward information on baptisms, marriages and burials, Church of Ireland parish records very often include vestry books. These contain the minutes of the vestry meetings of the local parish, which can supply detailed information on the part played by individuals in the life of the parish. These are not generally with the parish registers in the National Archives of Ireland, but the Public Record Office of Northern Ireland and the Representative Church Body Library in Dublin have extensive collections.

Where are Church of Ireland records?

1. *The National Archives of Ireland.* Early Church of Ireland records are still legally public records and the Archives, as the successor to the old Public Record Office, should have custody of them. Perhaps due to the experience of the first round of custody ending in 1922, the Archives now hold microfilm copies. The most up-to-date account is in the Archives' catalogue of Church of Ireland records, available in the reading room at the National Library, and in *A Table of Church of Ireland Parochial Records* (ed. Noel Reid, IFHS, 4th ed., 2001).
2. *The Public Record Office of Northern Ireland.* For the northern counties of Antrim, Armagh, Cavan, Derry, Donegal, Down, Fermanagh, Leitrim, Louth, Monaghan and Tyrone, surviving registers have been microfilmed by the Public Record Office of Northern Ireland and are available to the public in Belfast. The *Guide to Church Records: Public*

Record Office of Northern Ireland (PRONI, 1994) gives details.

3. *The Representative Church Body Library (RCBL).* The Church of Ireland's main repository for its archives and manuscripts now holds the original records from some 800 parishes in the Republic of Ireland. For those counties that are now in the Republic — Cavan, Donegal, Leitrim, Louth and Monaghan — copies of PRONI microfilms are available to the public at the RCBL.
4. *Local custody.* For a decreasing number of parishes the registers are still in local custody and you have to ask the local clergyman to search them. The current *Church of Ireland Directory* will supply the relevant name and address, and the suggested donation.

PRESBYTERIAN RECORDS

Dates

Presbyterian registers generally start much later than those of the Church of Ireland, though in areas which had a strong Presbyterian population from an early date, particularly in Antrim and Down, some registers date from the late seventeenth and early eighteenth centuries. Before registers were kept, Presbyterian baptisms, marriages and deaths are often to be found in the registers of the local

Church of Ireland parish. The only published listing is still in Margaret Falley's *Irish and Scotch-Irish Ancestral Research* (repr. Genealogical Publishing Co., 1988) which gives a very incomplete and out of date picture of the records. For the six counties of Northern Ireland and many of the adjoining counties the *Guide to Church Records: Public Record Office of Northern Ireland* (PRONI, 1994), also online at the PRONI website, provides a good guide to the dates of surviving registers. The copy of the list held in the Office itself includes a listing of registers in local custody which covers all of Ireland but is much less comprehensive for the South than for the North.

What Presbyterian records contain

Presbyterian registers record the same information as that given in the registers of the Church of Ireland (see above). It should be remembered that after 1845 all non-Catholic marriages, including those of Presbyterians, were registered by the state. From that year therefore Presbyterian marriage registers contain all the invaluable information given in state records.

Where are Presbyterian records?

Presbyterian registers are in three main locations: in local custody, in the Public Record Office of Northern Ireland, and at the Presbyterian

Historical Society in Belfast. The Public Record Office also has microfilm copies of almost all registers in Northern Ireland that have remained in local custody, and also lists those records held by the Presbyterian Historical Society. For the rest of Ireland, almost all the records are in local custody. It can be difficult to locate these since many congregations in the South have moved, amalgamated or simply disappeared over the last sixty years. The very congregational basis of Presbyterianism further complicates matters, since it means that Presbyterian records do not cover a definite geographical area; the same town often had two or more Presbyterian churches drawing worshippers from the same community but keeping distinct records. In the early nineteenth century especially, controversy within the Church fractured the records, with intense opposition between seceding and non-seceding congregations in the same area. Apart from the PRONI listing, the only guide is *A History of Congregations in the Presbyterian Church*, currently out of print, which gives a brief historical outline of the history of each congregation. Lewis's *Topographical Dictionary of Ireland* (1837) records the existence of Presbyterian congregations within each civil parish.

QUAKER RECORDS

The Society of Friends, or Quakers, kept wonderful records. There are two main repositories for these: the libraries of the Society of Friends in Dublin and Lisburn. The LDS library in Salt Lake City has microfilm copies of the records of the Dublin Friends' library. In addition to births, marriages and deaths, these also contain considerable collections of letters, wills and family papers, as well as detailed accounts of the discrimination suffered by Quakers in their early years. The National Library has microfilm copies of most of the Dublin and Lisburn libraries' holdings (Pos. 1021–4, Pos. 4125–7 and Pos. 5530–1).

OTHER DENOMINATIONS

Methodism, as a movement rather than a Church, gave its members a great deal of latitude in their attitude to Church membership, so that records of the baptisms, marriages and burials of Methodists may also be found in Quaker, Presbyterian or Church of Ireland registers. In addition the ministers of the Church were preachers on a circuit, rather than administrators of a particular area, and were moved frequently from one circuit to another. Quite often the records moved with them. For the nine historic counties of Ulster, the Public Record Office of Northern Ireland has produced a county-by-county listing of the surviving registers, their dates and locations, appended to their Parish Register index. No such listing exists for the rest of the country. Pettigrew and Oulton's *Dublin Almanac and General Register of Ireland* of 1835 (and subsequent years) provides a list of Methodist preachers and their stations, which will give an indication of the relevant localities. The next step then is to identify the closest surviving Methodist centre and enquire of them as to surviving records. Many of the local county heritage centres also hold indexed copies of surviving Methodist records.

FIVE

PROPERTY RECORDS

Census and church records, along with the state birth, marriage and death registers, are the only Irish sources specifically designed to record family information. From here on all your research will be on material created for other purposes in which any family information is incidental — not quite the bottom of the barrel, but on the way.

The townland is a peculiarly Irish phenomenon. At its simplest a townland is an area of rural land perceived as a unit by the people living there. This is a long, long way from postcode mathematical precision, and in fact the size of a townland can vary hugely, from a few small fields to more than a thousand acres. The townland was and is the basic unit of a rural address in Ireland. Since the vast majority of the population was rural until very recently, a townland address is one of the most important, if not the single most important goal of Irish research. Up to the end of the nineteenth century townlands were organised into civil parishes, almost identical to Church of Ireland parishes, and used as the basis of local administration and therefore local records. The standard reference work, the *Townlands Index*, is based on the 1851 census records and lists more than 60,000 townland names. It is available online at **www.ireland.com/ancestor** and **www.seanruad.com.**

GRIFFITH'S VALUATION

By far the most widely used and easily available Irish source is the *General Valuation of Rateable Property in Ireland*, known as 'Griffith's Valuation' after Sir Richard Griffith who supervised its creation. Its aim was to produce a consistent valuation of all the property in the country in order to provide for a uniform system of local taxation, and in this respect Griffith was extraordinarily successful. The Valuation Office (still in existence) produced the results between 1847 and 1864 in a series of volumes arranged by county, barony, Poor Law Union, civil parish and townland, which list every landholder and householder in Ireland.

Apart from the townland or street address and the occupier's name, the particulars given are:

- a map reference
- the name of the person from whom the property was leased or rented (immediate lessor)

- a standardised description of the property
- the acreage, and
- separate valuations of buildings and land.

The only directly useful family information given is in areas where a surname was particularly common. When the surveyors were faced with more than one individual with the same Christian name and surname in the one townland, they often adopted the Gaelic practice of using the father's first name to distinguish between the individuals, so that 'John Brady (Patrick)' is the son of Patrick, while 'John Brady (Michael)' is the son of Michael. At times an occupation (fiddler or weaver for example) is cited; on the rare occasions when two women of the same name are recorded as occupiers — almost invariably widows — their maiden names might be used to distinguish them. Because the Valuation entries were subsequently revised at regular intervals, it is often possible to trace living descendants of those originally listed by Griffith (see the Valuation Office, below).

Although never intended as a census, the Valuation has acquired an unlikely significance because of the destruction of nineteenth-century censuses in 1922. As things stand, it gives the only detailed guide to where people lived and what property they possessed in mid-nineteenth-century Ireland.

Availability and indexes

- Copies of the Valuation are widely available in major libraries and record offices, generally on microfiche.
- The first quasi-index dates from the 1960s, a county-by-county series known as the 'Index of Surnames' or 'Householders' Index' which gives a count for each civil parish of the number of householders in the Valuation. A similar count (via database) is available at **www.ireland.com/ancestor.**
- Microfiche indexes, which list alphabetically all the householders in the Valuation and show the townland and civil parish in which the entry is recorded, have been produced by All-Ireland Heritage and are available in the National Library.
- A CD-ROM index to the entire Valuation was published in 1997 by Broderbund Software in association with Heritage World of Dungannon and the Genealogical Publishing Company. You should sup with a long spoon when using it. Large portions appear to be missing, including Limerick city and all surnames after 'L' in wide swathes of south Tipperary.
- An online subscription version is available from **www.otherdays.com.**
- Another online version, pay-per-view, is at **www.irishorigins.com.**

TITHE APPLOTMENT BOOKS

If Griffith's is an unlikely genealogical source, then the Tithe Applotment Books (or 'Tithe Books' as they are generally known) are thoroughly improbable. They are the result of the Composition Act of 1823 which specified that tithes due to the Church of Ireland, hitherto payable in kind, should now be paid in cash. It was then necessary to carry out a valuation of the entire country, civil parish by civil parish, to establish how much would be payable by each landholder. This was done over the following fifteen years, up to the final abolition of tithes in 1838. Not surprisingly tithes were fiercely resented by the ninety per cent of the population who were not members of the Church of Ireland, and all the more because the tax was not payable on all land; the patchwork of traditional exemptions produced spectacular inequalities.

Apart from the fact that they leave out all households not in occupation of land, certain categories of land varying from area to area are simply passed over in silence. They are most certainly not a full list of householders. However they do constitute the only countrywide survey for the period and are valuable precisely because the heaviest burden of tithes fell on the poorest, for whom few other records survive.

What Tithe Books contain

From a genealogical point of view the information recorded in the Tithe Books is quite basic, consisting typically of:

- the townland name
- the landholder's name
- the area of land, and
- the tithes payable.

In addition, many Books also record the landlord's name and an assessment of the economic productivity of the land; the tax was based on the average price of wheat and oats over the seven years up to 1823, and was levied at a different rate depending on the quality of the land.

Tithe defaulters

An organised campaign of resistance to the payment of tithes, the so-called 'Tithe War', culminated in 1831 in large-scale refusals to pay the tax. To apply for compensation for the resultant loss of income, local Church of Ireland clergymen were required to produce lists of anyone liable for tithes who had not paid, the 'tithe defaulters'. The lists can provide a fuller picture of tithe-payers than the original Tithe Book, and can be useful to cross-check against the Book, especially if it dates from before 1831. In the National Archives Chief Secretary's Office, Official

Papers series, 127 of these lists survive. They relate principally to Counties Kilkenny and Tipperary with some coverage also of Counties Carlow, Cork, Kerry, Laois, Limerick, Louth, Meath, Offaly, Waterford and Wexford. A full list was published in *The Irish Genealogist*, Vol. 8, No. 1, 1990. County-by-county microfiche indexes have been produced by Data Tree Publishing, **www.alphalink.com.au/~datatree**. These are available at the National Library of Ireland.

Availability and indexes

- Microfilm copies of the Tithe Books are available in the National Archives and the National Library.
- Microfilm copies for the nine counties of Ulster are available in the Public Record Office of Northern Ireland.
- The LDS Family History Library has microfilm copies of the full series.
- A CD-Rom index for Counties Antrim, Armagh, Derry, Down, Fermanagh and Tyrone was published in 1999 by Family Tree Maker.
- The Index of Surnames or Householders' Index includes an indication of whether a surname appears in a particular parish.

The usefulness of the Tithe Books can vary enormously. Since they only give names, with no indication of family relationships, any conclusions drawn are speculative; but for parishes where church records do not begin until after 1850 they can be the only early records surviving. Valuable circumstantial evidence can sometimes emerge from them, for example where a holding passed from father to son in the period between the Tithe survey and Griffith's Valuation.

THE VALUATION OFFICE

The Valuation Office, set up to carry out the original primary valuation, is still in existence and has two related sets of records that are potentially valuable. The first of these are the notebooks used by the original Valuation surveyors, consisting of 'field books', 'house books' and 'tenure books'. All three record a map reference for the holdings they deal with, as in the published Valuation. The field books record information on the size and quality of the holding; the house books record the occupiers' names and the measurements of any buildings on their holdings; and the tenure books give the annual rent paid and the legal basis on which the holding is occupied, whether by lease or at will. The tenure books also give the year of any lease, useful to know before searching estate papers or the Registry of Deeds. As well as containing information such as this, which does not appear in the published Valuation, the valuers' notebooks can also be useful in documenting any changes in occupation between the initial survey and the published results, for instance if a family emigrated in the years immediately before publication, since they pre-date the final publication itself by several years. Unfortunately they are not extant for all areas. The National Archives now houses those that survive for the Republic of Ireland. Those covering Northern Ireland are now to be found in the Public Record Office of Northern Ireland.

The Valuation Office also holds the 'Cancelled Land Books' and 'Current Land Books' which give details of all changes in the holdings from the time of the primary valuation up to the present day. Any variations in the size or status of the holding, the names of the occupier or lessor, or the valuation itself are given in the revisions carried out every few years. The books can be useful in pinpointing a possible date of death or emigration or in identifying a living relative. A large majority of those who were in occupation of a holding by the 1890s, when the Land Acts began to subsidise the purchase of the land by its tenant farmers, have descendants or relatives still living in the same area.

The Cancelled Land Books for Northern Ireland are now in the Public Record Office of Northern Ireland. The LDS Family History Library has microfilm copies of the Valuation Office books.

Unfortunately the films are in black and white, while the amendments to the books are colour coded.

ESTATE RECORDS

Estate records really should be well down the list of research sources because they are difficult to use and they produce results only in a small minority of cases. Their existence is due to the fact that up to the end of the nineteenth century the vast majority of the Irish population lived as small tenant farmers on large estates owned for the most part by English or Anglo-Irish landlords. The administration of these estates produced large quantities of records — maps, tenants' lists, rentals, account books, lease books etc. Over the course of the twentieth century as the estates have been broken up and sold off, many collections of these records have found their way into public repositories.

Because of the size of the estates, it was quite rare for a large landowner to have individual rental or lease agreements with the huge numbers of small tenants on his land. Instead he would let a significant area to a middleman who would then sublet to others, who might in turn rent out parts to the smallest tenants. So it is very rare for estate records to document the smallest landholders.

The largest collections are in the two major Dublin repositories, the National Archives and the National Library, and in the Public Record Office of Northern Ireland, but there are Irish estate papers in English County record offices and archives, in Irish county libraries and museums, and some still in private hands. The sole comprehensive guide is Richard Hayes's 'Manuscript Sources for the Study of Irish Civilization' and its supplements, copies of which can be found in major libraries. This catalogues the records by landlord's name and by county, which means that this is the minimum information you need to find a relevant collection.

Only the PRONI collection is fully catalogued in sufficient detail to make research focused on particular areas feasible. For the National Library and National Archives a more detailed guide to the dates, areas covered and class of tenants recorded is in preparation by the National Library in association with the Irish Genealogical Society of Minnesota — to date, Counties Armagh, Carlow, Cavan, Clare, Cork, Donegal, Fermanagh, Kerry, Kildare, Leitrim, Limerick, Galway, Mayo, Monaghan, Roscommon, Sligo, Tyrone, Waterford, Westmeath and Wicklow have been covered. The results are available at the Archives and in the Library genealogy room.

Like so many unlikely Irish sources, when

estate records do turn out to be relevant, they can be very rewarding, especially for the period before the major nineteenth-century surveys. To take one example, the Connolly estate in south Donegal has records from the early eighteenth century that record a large number of leases to smaller tenants, often specifying family relationships. But the majority of the rentals and tenants' lists only give details of major tenants.

SIX

TRADE DIRECTORIES

Like many sources for Irish genealogy, when directories are good they're very, very good, and when they're bad they're horrid. The main problem is that they cover only very specific areas and classes of people. Until the end of the nineteenth century they include only towns and they always exclude small tenant farmers, servants and landless labourers, the vast majority of our ancestors, in other words.

This much said, for town-dwellers, however modest, they can provide superb information. The very least a directory entry can show is precisely where a family lived at the time the entry was made. The further up the social scale you go, through traders, merchants, professionals and gentry, the more they reveal. Followed over a series of years — particularly in the Dublin and Belfast directories — the entries can show growing or declining prosperity, and they provide evidence of death, inheritance, family connections and emigration.

When using directories, remember:

- the entries were usually six months out of date by the time of publication

- with an arrogance which is still familiar, the publishers of Dublin directories tended to confuse Dublin with Ireland and included many individuals in rural areas well outside the capital
- like all sources, they do contain mistakes.

Because trade directories relate directly to specific areas, what you will find depends entirely on where your ancestors lived. The most comprehensive are those for Dublin, followed by some of the provincial publications and those that attempt to cover the entire island. In general the information given below only goes as far as the end of the nineteenth century.

DUBLIN DIRECTORIES

The earliest Irish directories are those published by Peter Wilson for Dublin city, starting in 1751 and continuing until 1837 with a break from 1754–9. Generally bound with John Watson's *Almanack* and the *English Court Registry* until it ceased publication in 1837, it was known as *The Treble Almanack*.

The information supplied by Wilson's *Directory* grew steadily, from the early alphabetical lists of merchants and traders, supplying names, addresses and occupations, to the inclusion of separate lists of officers of the city guilds and officers of Trinity

College, state officials, those involved in the administration of medicine and the law, and Church of Ireland clergy. Some intermittent appearances from the early nineteenth century include pawnbrokers, bankers, apothecaries, police, dentists, physicians, militia officers and ships' captains.

Pettigrew and Oulton's *Dublin Almanac and General Register of Ireland* began annual publication in 1834 and saw the first street-by-street listing, initially only of the inhabitants of Dublin city, but growing year by year to encompass the suburbs. The 1835 edition added an alphabetical list of the individuals recorded in the street listings. The combination of the two listings should make it possible to track the movements of individuals around the city, an important feature since urban households moved frequently in the nineteenth century. However the alphabetical list is actually much less comprehensive than the street list.

Pettigrew and Oulton also extended the range of persons covered. As well as clergy and the officials of almost every Dublin institution, private and public, they broadened their coverage to areas outside Dublin supplying the names of many of the rural gentry and more prosperous inhabitants of the large towns. In effect these are mini-directories themselves, especially useful for rural towns without surviving directories in their own right.

- 1824 onwards gives separate alphabetical listings for the clergy, gentry and nobility of Dublin and most of the larger urban centres.
- 1824 includes a countrywide alphabetical index to all the clergy, gentry and nobility listed in the entries for individual towns, which was omitted in subsequent issues.
- 1846 includes the names of schoolteachers for the towns treated, a practice continued in subsequent editions.
- 1881 supplies the names of the principal farmers near each of the towns treated, giving the relevant parish. This feature was continued in the 1894 edition.

The best single collection of these directories is in the National Library where most of the early editions have now been transferred to microfiche.

Provincial directories

John Ferrar's *Directory of Limerick*, published in 1769, was the first directory to deal specifically with a provincial town, and the practice spread throughout Munster in the remaining decades of the eighteenth century, with Cork particularly well covered. In the nineteenth century local directories were produced in abundance, especially in areas with a strong commercial identity such as Belfast and the north-east and, again, Munster. The quality and coverage of these varies widely, from the street-by-street listings in Martin's 1839 *Belfast Directory* to the barest of commercial lists.

Some guides:
James Carty, *National Library of Ireland Bibliography of Irish History 1870–1911*, Dublin, 1940.

Edward Evans, *Historical and Bibliographical Account of Almanacks, Directories etc. in Ireland from the Sixteenth Century*, Dublin, 1897 (Facsimile ed. Blackrock, Carraig Books, 1976).

M. E. Keen, *A Bibliography of Trade Directories of the British Isles in the Victoria and Albert Museum*, London, 1979.

Microfilm copies of many of the directories are available for purchase online. See **www.vinehall.com.au**.

SEVEN

OCCUPATIONS

ARMY/MILITIA

How you proceed depends on whether your ancestor was a soldier or an officer and on the period in which they served. Almost all the records are in the English Public Record Office (PRO).

Soldiers

From the late eighteenth century on, a very large proportion of the rank and file of the British Army consisted of Irishmen: one estimate for the mid-nineteenth century is forty per cent of the total. You should remember that these men served throughout the army and not exclusively in the Irish regiments.

Soldiers' documents

WO 97, which contains records of discharges from the army between 1760 and 1913, can often provide details of place of birth, age and appearance and, after 1882, next of kin. The records up to 1882 only cover soldiers discharged to pension; after that year all discharges are recorded. Before 1873 the records are organised by regiment, but a name index exists for the period 1760 to 1854. Between 1854 and 1873 you must know the regiment to use the records. From 1873 to 1882 they are organised under the collective headings Artillery, Cavalry, Corps and Infantry, and then alphabetically under these headings. From 1883 they are alphabetical.

> NOTE. Only a minority of soldiers were discharged to pension. If your soldier does not appear in the Soldiers' Documents, you may find him in one of the sources below.

Pension records

If a soldier was discharged to pension or discharged as medically unfit in Ireland before 1823, detailed information will be found in the registers of the Royal Hospital, Kilmainham (WO 119), containing the Certificates of Service. These are organised by regimental number which you can trace through WO 118, Kilmainham Admission Books. In-pensioners' records (those actually resident in the institution) go from 1704 to 1922 and are also in WO 118. Irish out-pensioners (those receiving a pension but not actually resident) were administered from the Royal Hospital, Chelsea, after 1822 (WO 116/117). Regimental registers of admissions to pension also exist, indexed from 1806 to 1836; otherwise each regimental volume includes an index. The National Archives of Ireland also has microfilm copies of the Kilmainham records.

You should remember:

- It was quite common for Irishmen to be discharged outside Ireland, in which case pension papers would be in the Chelsea records, even between 1760 and 1822.
- Only a minority of those who served are covered.

Pay lists and musters

Each regiment made a quarterly return of all personnel from the early eighteenth century to 1878. From the 1860s these also included details of wives and children living in married quarters. These are obviously much more comprehensive than the pensions and discharge records and can supply fascinating details about individuals. The date of enlistment can be used to search the relevant muster, which should give birthplace, age and former occupation. The records are in WO 10, 11, 12 and 13. It is necessary to know the regiment before using these records.

Other records

Casualties and deserters

Soldiers who died on active service are recorded in the regimental returns of casualties from 1795 to 1875 in WO 25 and are indexed. Additional material such as wills, lists of effects or details of next of kin may also be found. The same series also includes details of absentees and registers of deserters for the first half of the nineteenth century. There is also an incomplete card index at the PRO for army deserters (1689–1830).

Description books

Also in WO 25 are the regimental description books, the earliest from 1756, the latest from 1900, which give physical details as well as a service history. They are not comprehensive and do not cover the entire period.

Regimental registers of births (1761–1924)

The index to regimental registers of births, 1761–1924, gives the regiment and place of birth of children born to the wives of serving soldiers, if they were attached to the regiment. The index is available at the PRO, but the records are held by the Family Records Centre and are not on open access.

Finding the Regiment

For most of the pre-1873 records, knowing the regiment is vital. It can be quite difficult.

- Uniforms. Try **www.regiments.org** or D. J. Barnes, 'Identification and Dating: Military Uniforms' in *Family History in Focus,* D. J. Steel and L. Taylor eds, (Guildford, 1984) or the National Army

Museum **www.national-army-museum.ac.uk.**

- The Regimental Registers of Births (see above) can help if you have some idea of the names of the children or the areas in which a soldier served.
- Wills of soldiers who died overseas were proved at the Prerogative Court of Canterbury (PROB 11). There are various published indexes. The registers of next of kin in WO 25 may also be useful.
- If you have an idea where a soldier was stationed, and approximately when, J. M. Kitzmiller's *In Search of the Forlorn Hope: a Comprehensive Guide to Locating British Regiments and their Records* (Salt Lake City, 1988) will help you locate where various regiments were stationed.

Later records

The Irish Soldier's & Sailor's Fund

This fund was set up to provide cottages for Irishmen who had served in the armed forces during World War I and helped build over 4,000 cottages up to the 1930s. In Northern Ireland cottages were built up to 1952. The records are organised by place; there is no name index. The tenancy files are in AP 7.

Boer War

The Family Record Centre has separate indexes to the deaths of army personnel in the South African (Boer) War from 1899 to 1902. The General Register Office in Dublin also has an index to 'Deaths of Irish Subjects pertaining to the South African War (1899–1902)' in the deaths index for 1902. Certified copies of the original entries include regiment and rank.

World War I

Of the six and a half million records of servicemen in World War I originally held at the War Office Record Store, more than four million were destroyed during World War II. Those that survived were charred or suffered water damage and were consequently unavailable for research. A microfilming project to make the records (generally known as the 'burnt documents') publicly accessible was completed in the summer of 2002, and the films are now available at the PRO and via LDS family history centres. More than two million individuals are covered, with a variety of records. Among the most common are attestation papers which give information about name, address, date of birth and next of kin.

Ireland's Memorial Records (Dublin, 1923) is an eight-volume commemorative publication listing the Irish men and women killed during the war and those of other nationalities who died while serving with Irish regiments. It also supplies the place of origin.

The Commonwealth War Graves Commission

The commission maintains graves in more than 150 countries covering approximately 925,000 individuals, members of the forces of the Commonwealth killed in the two world wars. Their website at **www.cwgc.org** includes extensive details on those buried.

Officers

Lists

The official *Army List* was published at least annually from 1740 and records all officers. *Hart's Army List*, which was published from 1839 to 1915, supplies more information about individuals' army careers. Both publications are available at the Public Record Office. Annotated copies, sometimes including supplementary details, are in WO 65 (1754–1879) and WO 66 (1879–1900).

Commissions

Records concerning the purchase and sale of the commissions of Irish officers from 1768 to 1871 can be found in HO 123. Correspondence relating to commissions generally between 1793 and 1871 is in WO 31. The records, arranged chronologically, can be extremely informative and are relatively simple to use since the date of commission is supplied by the *Army List*.

Service records

These records, in WO 25, are not comprehensive, consisting of a series of surveys carried out every fifteen to twenty years between 1809 and 1872. The early returns concentrate on military service, with some biographical detail supplied in the later ones. The records are covered by an alphabetical card index on open access which also takes in WO 75, an episodic series of regimental service returns between 1755 and 1954.

Pensions

Up to 1871, if an officer did not sell his commission on retirement, he went on half-pay, a retainer that meant he was theoretically available for service. Records of these payments, as well as widows' and dependents' pensions, can provide detailed biographical information. The half-pay ledgers of payment from 1737 to 1921 are in PMG 4, arranged by regiment up to 1841 and thereafter alphabetically. WO 25 also contains much detail on pensions and dependents.

Others

Many officers' original baptismal certificates are included in War Office records for 1777–1868 in

WO 32/8903 to WO 32/8920 (code 21A) and for 1755–1908 in WO 42. Both are indexed.

ATTORNEYS AND BARRISTERS

Up to 1867 it was necessary to be admitted to the King's Inns Society to become either a barrister or attorney (solicitor). Roman Catholics were excluded until 1794. To gain admission to the society as either an apprentice (to become a solicitor) or a student (to become a barrister) a good deal of family information had to be submitted. The earlier papers relating to admissions are incomplete, but what survives has been published in *King's Inns Admission Papers, 1607–1867*, edited by Edward Keane, P. Beryl Phair and Thomas U. Sadlier (Dublin: Stationery Office for the Irish Manuscripts Commission, 1982).

To follow the later careers of lawyers, directories, in particular Dublin directories, are the major source.

CLERGYMEN

Roman Catholic

Since Roman Catholic priests did not marry, their usefulness for genealogical research is limited, but their relative prominence means they left records that can lead to information on other members of their families. Obituaries are relatively common from the latter half of the nineteenth century and the information in their seminary records can help identify a precise place of origin.

Until the 1790s all Irish Catholic clergy were educated in continental Europe because of the legal restrictions of the penal laws. When these were lifted, two seminaries were founded in short order, St Patrick's in Carlow and St Patrick's in Maynooth. Some of the records of both have been published:

- *Maynooth Students and Ordinations Index, 1795–1895* (Patrick J. Hamell, Birr, Co. Offaly, 1992).
- *Carlow College 1793–1993: the Ordained Students and the Teaching Staff of St Patrick's College, Carlow* (J. McEvoy, Carlow, St Patrick's College, 1993).

The *Irish Catholic Directory*, published annually since 1836, lists priests by diocese and parish.

Church of Ireland

Biographical details of Church of Ireland clergy can be found in the Leslie Biographical Index, a far-reaching compendium originated by the Rev. James Leslie and held at the Representative Church Body Library in Dublin. Additional information is also available in Leslie's succession lists, chronological accounts arranged by diocese and parish. The succession lists for thirteen dioceses have been published. The RCBL has these and the remaining dioceses in typescript.

Church of Ireland directories were also published intermittently but frequently in the first half of the nineteenth century, and annually from 1862.

Methodist

The key work for Methodist clergy is *An Alphabetical Arrangement of all the Wesleyan Methodist Preachers and Missionaries (Ministers, Missionaries & Preachers on Trial) etc.* (Bradford T. Inkersley), originally by William Hill but republished twenty-one times between 1819 and 1927. It covers all clergy in the British Isles, giving locations and year of service.

C. H. Crookshank's *History of Methodism in Ireland, 1740–1860* (3 Vols, Belfast, 1885–8) records brief biographical details of preachers. It is continued in H. Lee Cole's *History of Methodism in Ireland, 1860–1960* (Belfast, 1961).

Presbyterian

Two works cover almost all ministers. The Rev. James McConnell's *Fasti of the Irish Presbyterian Church 1613–1840* (Belfast, 1938) covers the early years of the Synod of Ulster. John M. Barkly's *Fasti of the General Assembly of the Presbyterian Church in Ireland 1840–1910* (3 Vols, Presbyterian Historical Society, 1986–7) takes things up to 1910.

DOCTORS

Because medical practice was only partly regulated before the mid-nineteenth century, early records of medical education are patchy. The major Irish institutions were the Dublin Guild of Barber-Surgeons (from 1576), the Royal College of Physicians of Ireland (from 1667), the Royal College of Surgeons in Ireland (from 1784) and Apothecaries Hall (from 1747). In addition, Dublin University (Trinity College) had a School of Physic (Medicine) from 1711. Many Irish medical men also trained in Britain or on the Continent.

The Dublin Guild of Barber-Surgeons' records are in Trinity College (Ms. 1447) and the Royal College of Physicians of Ireland has registers from the seventeenth century. However both sources are difficult to access and use. In most cases Dublin directories or Freeman's Lists are just as informative and easier to use. The records of Apothecaries Hall from 1747 to 1833 are on microfilm in the National Library (Pos. 929). *Alumni Dublinenses* (G.D. Burtchaell and T.U. Sadlier eds, Dublin, 1935) contains detailed records of Trinity students up to 1860.

To trace the careers of medical practitioners, the major sources are Dublin directories, which list physicians and surgeons from 1761 and apothecaries from 1751, local (generally later) directories (see Chapter 6) and Irish Medical directories, published intermittently between 1843 and the end of the nineteenth century.

Another less conventional source is the 'Biographical file on Irish medics' compiled by T. P. C. Kirkpatrick, a compendium of biographical material on Irish medics up to 1954 and held in the Royal College of Physicians. The college and the National Library both hold a copy of the index.

POLICEMEN

From the late eighteenth century a police force operated in Dublin city, with a part-time *ad hoc* constabulary in the rest of the country. In 1814 an armed Peace Preservation Force was created, followed in 1822 by the full-time County Constabulary. These two were amalgamated in 1836 into the Irish Constabulary, and renamed the Royal Irish Constabulary (better known as the RIC) in 1867. The separate Dublin force which remained in existence was known as the Dublin Metropolitan Police (DMP). With the creation of the Irish Free State in 1922 the RIC was disbanded. Responsibility for policing passed to the Garda Síochána in the twenty-six counties, and to the newly formed Royal Ulster Constabulary in the six counties of Northern Ireland.

Excellent personnel records were kept from 1816. The General Register from that date to 1922 is now in the Public Record Office, Kew (HO 184), with microfilm copies in the National Archives of Ireland, the LDS Family History Library and the Public Record Office of Northern Ireland. For each recruit it includes a brief service record, date of marriage and wife's native county, and the name of the individual who recommended him. This can be important in helping to identify an exact place of origin, since the recommendations usually came from local clergymen or magistrates who knew the recruit personally. Thom's Directories (see Chapter 6) can pinpoint their address. HO 184 also comprises a separate Officers' Register.

The partly alphabetical index to the registers included in HO 184 has now been superseded by Jim Herlihy's *The Royal Irish Constabulary: a Complete Alphabetical List of Officers and Men, 1816–1922* (Dublin: Four Courts, 1999), which supplies the service number needed to use the registers efficiently.

A further source, available only at Kew, is PMG 48, 'Pensions and allowances to officers, men and staff of the Royal Irish Constabulary and to their widows and children'. This dates from the 1870s and usually gives the address of the recipient.

The DMP Register is held by the Garda Archives at Dublin Castle but is more readily available on microfilm at the National Archives. It does not give marriage details but supplies a parish of origin.

TEACHERS

Irish education was relatively informal until quite recently. Until the last quarter of the nineteenth century a large majority of Irish teachers had no training.

The Society for Promoting the Education of the Poor of Ireland, better known as the Kildare Place Society, was the first attempt to provide systematic non-denominational primary education. Founded in 1811, it trained several thousand teachers and supported schools throughout the country. Its personnel records from 1814 to 1854 are now held by the Church of Ireland College of Education in Dublin.

Appendix 22 of the *Irish Education Enquiry, 1826, 2nd Report* (4 Vols) lists all the parochial schools in Ireland in 1824, including the names of teachers and other details. It is indexed in

Schoolmasters and Schoolmistresses in Ireland, 1826–1827 by Dorothy Rines Dingfelder (National Library, Ir. 372 d 38).

The enquiry itself was set up because of the objections of the Roman Catholic hierarchy to the non-denominational nature of the Kildare Place schools. Its outcome was the establishment of the Board of National Education in 1831, which ended state support for Kildare Place schools and placed control of elementary education in the hands of the local clergy in the form of national schools, a system that is still in place.

The principal source for teachers in the national schools is the series of Teachers' Salary Books from 1834 to 1855 held by the National Archives. These are not particularly informative from a genealogical point of view, but they sometimes include comments that can be of interest. They are organised by school, so it is necessary to know where your teacher was working.

EIGHT

THE INTERNET

Genealogy and computers were made for each other. The Internet holds out the promise of transforming genealogical research. For many areas outside Ireland the promise is already coming good — witness the Scottish General Register Office, **www.scotlandspeople.gov.uk**, or the 1901 census for England and Wales, **www.census.pro.gov.uk**. Unfortunately in the case of Irish research the change has been slow and piecemeal with, as is so often the case in Ireland, narrow sectional interests outweighing the common good. Few of the institutions holding records have even begun the process of making them available online and what records there are can be variable in quality.

None the less the huge interest in Irish genealogy, particularly in North America, has produced a profusion of resources for anyone with Irish ancestors. The survey that follows presumes only familiarity with the basics of World Wide Web browsers and email.

> Websites, especially small personal sites that may contain invaluable family record details, are very perishable. If you cannot find one that you know used to be there, the Internet Archive Project, **web.archive.org**, almost

certainly has a stored copy. Their 'Wayback machine' stores copies of virtually all sites that have appeared (and disappeared) since 1998 and is readily searchable.

STARTING POINTS

Although the Internet may change the ways the sources can be used, the fact is that the Internet has not added any new sources. For this reason it is a good idea to be aware of what the original sources are. Few sites attempt to describe the sources, the information they record and how that information can be interpreted. There are two kinds of starting points: general guides to Irish research, and guides to Irish-interest Internet sites.

Research guides

Good basic guides can be found at the National Archives of Ireland site, **www.nationalarchives.ie/genealogy.html**, and the National Library of Ireland site, **www.nli.ie/pdfs/famil1.pdf.** A more detailed treatment can be found on a site in which I have a personal involvement, Irish Ancestors, part of the Irish Times ireland.com site, **www.ireland.com/ancestor**. The 'Browse' section gives detailed accounts of all the record sources used in Irish research.

Other brief guides include:

- Sean Murphy's Beginner's Guide, **homepage.eircom.net/~seanjmurphy/dir/guide.htm**, and
- The Fianna Homepage, **www.rootsweb.com/~fianna**, which presumes research is being done via the Family History centres of the Church of Jesus Christ of Latter-Day Saints.

Listings sites

There are numerous listings sites which provide links to Irish genealogy sites. Since many of these themselves largely consist of listings, a frustrating amount of travelling in circles is inevitable. The sites given below are the largest and most stable. For a more detailed treatment of the structure of the first two in particular, see Peter Christian's *The Genealogist's Internet* (Public Record Office, 2001), by far the most comprehensive publication on genealogy and the Internet. Of their nature all these sites suffer from a certain amount of link-rot.

- The 'mother of all' genealogy site lists is Cyndi Howell's **www.cyndislist.com** which categorises and cross-references online genealogical resources. The Irish section is at **www.cyndislist.com/ireland.htm**. With over 175,000 links in total the sheer scale of the enterprise is impressive, but it is also the site's main weakness: it can be almost as difficult to track something down on Cyndi's List as it is on the Internet itself.

- A more discriminating guide can be found at Genuki, **www.genuki.org.uk/indexes/IRLcontents.html**, where a good attempt is made to give a comprehensive overview of the relevant records, with links listed where there are matching online resources.
- The WorldGenWeb project is a volunteer-run survey of sources relating to particular localities. The county-by-county listings for the twenty-six counties now in the Republic can be found at **www.irelandgenweb.com** and those for the six counties of Northern Ireland at **www.rootsweb.com/~nirwgw**. The quality of the listings depends very much on the enthusiasm and discrimination of the individuals responsible. Leprechauns are a constant hazard.
- The Irish Ancestors listings at **scripts.ireland.com/ancestor/browse/links** attempt to present a county-by-county listing of what source materials are available, as well as passenger lists and family sites.

Other sites with valuable listings include:

- **irelandgenealogyprojects.rootsweb.com**: similar to the WorldGenWeb project but for Ireland only.

- **www.genealogylinks.net/uk/ireland**: a good listing despite the identification of Ireland as a region of the UK.
- **www.tiara.ie/links.html**: another well-maintained and comprehensive site, that of the Irish Ancestral Research Association.
- **www.doras.ie**: the Irish telecom company Eircom has a very large directory of Irish sites which includes an extensive listing of Irish surname and family sites, as well as many Irish genealogy sites. Unusually a rating system is used in an attempt to give some idea of the quality of the sites listed. Unfortunately no categorisation other than 'genealogy' is used, which can make it difficult to pin down specifics.

SOURCES ONLINE

As already outlined, there are few sites offering comprehensive searches of Irish sources. But for particular areas and records there are some very good sites, giving a tantalising glimpse of the way things should be.

Major sources

General Register Office Records

The Republic GRO website is at **www.groireland.ie** and the Northern Ireland office is at **www.groni.gov.uk.** Neither has an online search facility. Although a government computerisation project has been in train for some years, its focus is primarily on facilitating the work of the Irish legal, health and welfare systems, with historical use well down the list of priorities. However the fact that the LDS Church has microfilm copies of most of the records has allowed a certain amount of piecemeal transcription to take place. It should be remembered that the microfilm copies they transcribe are themselves transcriptions of local registrations, with the inevitable additional layer of human error.

- **www.familysearch.org.** The LDS site itself includes transcripts of the first five years of birth registrations, 1864–68, as part of the International Genealogical Index.
- **193.193.166.161/death.html.** Waterford County Library has made local death registrations available and freely searchable from 1864 to 1901.
- **www.clarelibrary.ie/eolas/coclare/genealogy/deaths_in_the_liscannor_area.htm.** Clare County Library has a list of deaths in the Liscannor area.
- **www.sci.net.au/userpages/mgrogan/cork.** Partial transcripts for Co. Cork are available on Margaret Grogan's site.

Quite a few sites invite users to submit records they have transcribed themselves. One of the best organised is **www.cmcrp.net**. The problems are self-evident: accuracy is always doubtful and in most cases it is not clear what proportion of the records is included.

Census records

There has been no systematic attempt to make either the 1901 or the 1911 census searchable online. The availability of the LDS microfilms for 1901 however has allowed transcriptions for particular areas. Only the most extensive transcripts are listed below. For county-by-county listings, see **www.census-online.com/links/Ireland/** and **scripts.ireland.com/ancestor/browse/links/counties.htm**, as well as **www.cyndislist.com/ireland.htm**.

- **www.leitrim-roscommon.com**. The best site for Irish census returns, indeed possibly the single best Irish research site on the Internet, is the Leitrim-Roscommon Genealogy website. As well as an almost complete database of the 1901 returns for Counties Leitrim and Roscommon, the site also contains large numbers of transcripts from Counties Mayo, Sligo, Westmeath and Wexford. Unlike many other sites, there is a systematic account of which records are complete and which are still to be added to. From my own experience, the quality of the transcripts is consistently good. I have certainly found records I had missed when searching the originals.

- **www.clarelibrary.ie**. Clare County Library has transcripts of the returns for 1901 for four out of the eight Poor Law Unions of the county.
- **www.sci.net.au/userpages/mgrogan/cork**. Margaret Grogan's site has a large number of transcripts for Cork for both 1901 and 1911 submitted by volunteers.
- **freepages.genealogy.rootsweb.com/~donegal /census.htm**: volunteer transcripts for 1901 and 1911 for parts of Donegal.
- **www.caora.net/find.php**: an index to the heads of households for Co. Down in 1901.

Parish records

Despite the fact that virtually all Irish parish records have been transcribed in database format, no systematic attempt has been made to make them searchable online. Anything online is once again largely a result of the availability of LDS microfilms to volunteer transcribers. Again, county-by-county listings are at **scripts.ireland.com /ancestor/browse/links/counties.htm** and a general listing is at **www.cyndislist.com/ireland.htm**.

- **www.familysearch.org**. The LDS website includes the records of twelve Roman Catholic parishes in Kerry and north-west Cork that were published by Albert Casey in *O'Kief, Coshe Mang* (16 Vols, pr.pr. 1964–72). As transcripts of transcripts, they need to be approached with caution.

- **www.rootsweb.com/~irllog/churchrecs.htm**, the records of five Longford Catholic parishes.
- **www.irishgenealogy.ie**. Irish Genealogy Ltd is a company set up to promote Irish genealogy. It currently offers a signposting database using the records of nine local heritage centres, which allows users to identify whether records matching their search criteria are held by the centre. This includes their parish register database transcripts. To access fuller details a commissioned search is then necessary.

Property records

Because of the lack of nineteenth-century census material the two property surveys, Griffith's Valuation (1847–64) and the Tithe Applotment Books (1823–38) have acquired unusual importance. Griffith's is the single most widely available source online.

- **www.otherdays.com**, a subscription site, has a fully indexed copy of the Valuation including page images from the original.
- **scripts.ireland.com/ancestor/surname** has a count of the number of Griffith's householders of a particular surname by county (free) and parish (paying).

- **www.leitrim-roscommon.com** has transcripts for twenty-two parishes in Roscommon, twenty-four in Limerick and ten in Galway.
- **www.irishorigins.com** includes a pay-per-view version of Griffith's, as well as a meta-search feature covering a vast number of sites which contain Irish genealogical material, including many of the sites listed here.

The Tithe Books are less well served. **www.caora.net** has an index to the Tithe Books of Co. Down. Otherwise **scripts.ireland.com/ancestor/browse/links/counties.htm** and **www.genealogylinks.net/uk/ireland** have county-by-county listings for individual parishes.

Other sources

Migration records

The vast majority of records relate to North America and Australia.

- **istg.rootsweb.com** is the exotically named Immigrant Ships Transcribers' Guild, the major site for ships' lists copied by volunteers, with the usual caveats.
- **www.ellisisland.org** is the Ellis Island site which has New York arrivals' records from 1892 to 1924.
- **scripts.ireland.com/ancestor/browse/links/passship-a.htm** has a selection of links to ships' lists.

- **www.nationalarchives.ie/search01.html** has an extensive but incomplete database of transportation records from Ireland to Australia up to 1868.
- **www.pcug.org.au/~ppmay/convicts.htm** has details of convict arrivals in Australia (1791–1820), a period for which the National Archives transportation registers have not survived.

Gravestone inscriptions

- **interment.net/ireland** provides webspace for 'everyday folks' to submit transcriptions and compilations. The site is well organised but very few of the transcripts are complete. The site is covered by the meta-search **www.irishorigins.com.**
- **www.fermanagh.org.uk**, Fermanagh Gold, has a good collection of Fermanagh gravestone inscriptions, as well as other information from the county.
- **www.webone.com.au/~sgrieves/cemetries_ireland.htm** has a good, reliable selection, mostly from Tipperary.

Military and police records

- **www.ancestry.com**, the largest commercial genealogy site, has very little of genuine interest for Ireland. One exception is the Royal Irish

Constabulary List, an index to the LDS microfilms of the original service registers. The index is about seventy per cent complete as of May 2003.

- **www.cwgc.org**, the Commonwealth War Graves Commission, is probably the best online military database.
- **www.greatwar.ie**, the Royal Dublin Fusiliers' Association, has excellent information on the Irish in World War I.

DISCUSSION GROUPS

Usenet

Discussion or news groups were among the first uses of the Internet and can still be extremely interesting. Most browsers now provide a newsreader, but the simplest means of access is through **groups.google.com**. The Irish group is **soc.genealogy.ireland**, which was set up in August 1997 — messages before that date will be in **soc.genealogy.uk+ireland**. Access is also provided by **www.irishinbritain.com**. A less widely used newsgroup, also available as above, is **soc.genealogy.surnames.ireland**.

Mailing lists

Mailing lists copy every message submitted to the group to all subscribed members. They can be useful for unusual surnames or specific research issues. Be sure to keep the initial instructions on how to unsubscribe or you may find yourself swamped. By far the largest and most venerable collection of lists is at **lists.rootsweb.com**. A full Irish list can be found at **www.rootsweb.com/~jfuller/gen_mail_country-unk-irl.html**. **groups.yahoo.com** has forty-six Irish genealogy lists.

GEOGRAPHY

The Holy Grail of Irish research is a specific townland address of origin. The 1851 Townlands Index, or more accurately *The General Alphabetical Index to the Townlands and Towns, Parishes and Baronies of Ireland* (repr. Genealogical Publishing Co., 1981), first published in 1861 and based on the 1851 census, is the standard source. It is freely searchable on two sites:

- **www.seanruad.com** has a straightforward interface and includes information on acreage and barony.
- **scripts.ireland.com/ancestor/placenames** allows wildcard searches and complete listings for individual parishes.

SURNAME SITES

Many who have done a good deal of research will publish it on a website, partly through altruism, partly through enlightened self-interest — the more people publish, the greater the chance that someone from a related branch of the family will see the information and be able to add to it. As always the information provided ranges from superb to abysmal. There are now millions of personal family history sites and tracking down any relevant ones can be difficult.

- **www.cyndislist.com** has an enormous list indexed alphabetically.
- **freepages.rootsweb.com** is the largest provider of free genealogy pages.
- **www.genealogy.com** also gives users free web pages and allows searches.
- **www.google.com**. A straightforward search on a site such as Google or Yahoo — 'Murphy Family History' — can often be surprisingly rewarding.

ARCHIVES AND LIBRARIES

The major repositories are:

- **www.nationalarchives.ie**, the National Archives of Ireland
- **www.nli.ie**, the National Library of Ireland

- **www.proni.gov.uk**, the Public Record Office of Northern Ireland
- **ireland.anglican.org/library**, the Representative Church Body Library.

Full contact details for local libraries can be found at **scripts.ireland.com/ancestor/browse/addresses.**

COMMISSIONING RESEARCH

- Both the National Library and the National Archives sites include lists of researchers willing to carry out commissioned research purely as a convenience
- **indigo.ie/~apgi** is the home site of the Association of Professional Genealogists in Ireland
- **www.irishroots.net** is the home of the Irish Family History Foundation, the umbrella body of the local heritage centre network in Ireland.

NINE

ADDRESSES

MAJOR REPOSITORIES (REPUBLIC OF IRELAND)

National Library of Ireland, Kildare St, Dublin 2
Tel: (01) 6030200, Fax: (01) 6766690
Email: **info@nli.ie**, Internet: **www.nli.ie**
Open 10–8.30 Mon, Tues, Wed; 10–4.30 Thurs, Fri; 10–12.30 Sat

National Archives of Ireland, Bishop St, Dublin 8
Tel: (01) 4072300, Fax: (01) 4072333
Email: **mail@nationalarchives.ie**
Internet: **www.nationalarchives.ie**
Open 10–5 Mon–Fri

General Register Office (Dublin), Joyce House, 8–11 Lombard St E., Dublin 2
Tel: (01) 6354000, Fax: (01) 6354440
Internet: **www.groireland.ie**
Open 9.30–12.30, 2.15–4.30 Mon–Fri

Land Valuation Office, Irish Life Centre, Abbey St Lower, Dublin 1
Tel: (01) 8171000, Fax: (01) 8171180
Email: **info@valoff.ie**, Internet: **www.valoff.ie**
Open 9.30–12.30, 2–4.30 Mon–Fri

Representative Church Body Library,
Braemor Park, Churchtown, Dublin 14
Tel: (01) 4923979, Fax: (01) 4924770
Email: **library@ireland.anglican.org**
Internet: **ireland.anglican.org/library/index.html**
Open 9–1, 1.45–5 Mon–Fri

Registry of Deeds, Henrietta St, Dublin 1
Tel: (01) 4733300
Internet: **www.irlgov.ie/landreg**
Open 10–4.30 Mon–Fri

Cork Archives Institute, Christ Church,
South Main St, Cork
Tel: (021) 4277809, Fax: (021) 4274668
Internet: **www.corkcity.ie/facilities/facilities_archive.html**
Open 10–1, 2.30–5 Tues–Fri

Society of Friends Library, Swanbrook House,
Morehampton Rd, Donnybrook, Dublin 4
Tel: (01) 6687157
Internet: **www.ipag.com/sites/quakers/index.html**
Open 10.30–1 Thurs

Family History Libraries (Latter-Day Saints)
Finglas Rd, Glasnevin, Dublin 11
Tel: (01) 8309960
Internet: **www.familysearch.org**
Open 7–9 pm Tues–Fri; 12.30–4.30 Thurs

Sarsfield Rd, Wilton, Cork
Tel: (021) 4341737
Open 10–12 Tues; 7–9 pm Wed

Dooradoyle Rd, Limerick
7–9 pm Fri

The Genealogical Office, 2 Kildare St, Dublin 2
Tel: (01) 6618811
Internet: **www.nli.ie/fr_offi2.htm**
Open 10–4.30 Mon–Fri

MAJOR REPOSITORIES (NORTHERN IRELAND)

Public Record Office of Northern Ireland, 66 Balmoral Avenue, Belfast BT9 6NY
Tel: (01232) 661621
Internet: **www.proni.gov.uk**
Open 9.15–4.45 Mon–Fri

Presbyterian Historical Society, Room 218, Church House, Fisherwick Place, Belfast BT1 6DW
Tel: (01232) 323936
Internet: **www.presbyterianireland.org/phsi/index.html**
Open 10–12.30 Mon–Fri; 10–12.30 and 2–4 Wed

Linen Hall Library, 17 Donegal Square North,
Belfast BT1 5GD
Tel: (01232) 321707, Fax: (01232) 438586
Internet: **www.linenhall.com**
Open 9.30–5.30 Mon–Fri; 9.30–4 Sat

General Register Office (Belfast), Oxford House,
49–55 Chichester St, Belfast BT1 4HL
Tel: (028) 90252000
Email: **gro.nisra@dfpni.gov.uk**
Internet: **www.groni.gov.uk**

Society of Friends Library (NI), Meeting House,
Railway St, Lisburn, Co. Antrim
Postal queries only

Family History Libraries (Latter-Day Saints),
8 Sandelfield, Coleraine, Co. Londonderry
Tel: (070) 321214
Internet: **www.familysearch.org**
Open 9.30–2.30 Tues; 6.30–8.30 pm Wed

403 Holywood Rd, Belfast
Tel: (00440) 2890768250
Internet: **www.familysearch.org**
Open 10–4 Wed, Thurs; 9–1 Sat

MAJOR REPOSITORIES (UK)

Family Records Centre, 1 Myddelton St, Islington
EC1R 1UW
Tel: (0870) 2437788, Fax: (0)1704550013
Email: **certificate.services@ons.gov.uk**
Internet: **www.familyrecords.gov.uk/frc**

Public Record Office, Kew, Richmond,
Surrey TW9 4DU
Tel: (020) 88763444, Fax: (020) 83925286
Internet: **www.pro.gov.uk**

HERITAGE CENTRES BY COUNTY

Antrim

Ulster Historical Foundation, 12 College Square
East, Belfast BT1 6DD
Tel: (028) 90332288, Fax: (028) 90239885
Email: **enquiry@uhf.org.uk**
Internet: **www.ancestryireland.co.uk**

Armagh

Armagh Ancestry, 38A English St, Armagh
BT61 7AB
Tel: (028) 37521802, Fax: (028) 37510033
Email: **ancestry@acdc.btinternet.com**
Internet: **www.irishroots.net/Armagh.htm**

Carlow

Carlow Genealogy Project, Old School, College St, Carlow
Tel: (0503) 30850
Recently reopened.

Cavan

Cavan Heritage and Genealogy Centre, Cana House, Farnham St, Cavan
Tel: (049) 4361094, Fax: (049) 4331494
Email: **canahous@iol.ie**
Internet: **www.irishroots.net/Cavan.htm**

Clare

Clare Genealogy Centre, Corofin, Co. Clare
Tel: (065) 6837955, Fax: (065) 6837540
Email: **clareheritage@eircom.net**
Internet: **clare.irish-roots.net**

Cork

Mallow Heritage Centre, 27–28 Bank Place, Mallow, Co. Cork
Tel: (022) 21778
Internet: **www.irishroots.net/Cork.htm**
North Cork only.

Cork city

Cork City Ancestral Project, c/o Cork County Library, Farranlea Rd, Cork
Tel: (021) 54699, Fax: (021) 343254

Derry

Derry/Londonderry Genealogy Centre, Heritage Library, 14 Bishop St, Derry BT48 6PW
Tel: (028) 71269792, Fax: (028) 71360921
Email: **ancestors@irelandmail.com**
Internet: **www.irishroots.net/Derry.htm**

Donegal

Donegal Ancestry, Old Meeting House, Back Lane, Ramelton, Co. Donegal
Tel: (074) 51266, Fax: (074) 51266
Email: **donances@indigo.ie**
Internet: **www.irishroots.net/Donegal.htm**

Down

See Antrim

Dublin

Dublin Heritage Group, 2nd Floor, Cumberland House, Fenian St, Dublin 2
Tel: (01) 4591048, Fax: (01) 6761628
Dublin city.

Fingal Heritage Project, The Carnegie Library, North St, Swords, Co. Dublin
Tel: (01) 8400080
Email: **swordsheritage@eircom.net**
Internet: **www.irishroots.net/Fingal.htm**
North Dublin only.

Dún Laoghaire-Rathdown Heritage Society, Moran Park House, Dún Laoghaire, Co. Dublin
Tel: (01) 2806961 Ext 238, Fax: (01) 2806969
Internet: **www.irishroots.net/DunLghre.htm**
South Dublin only.

Fermanagh

Heritage World, The Heritage Centre, 26 Market Sq., Dungannon BT70 1AB
Tel: (028) 87761306, Fax: (028) 87767663
Email: **irishwld@iol.ie**
Internet: **www.irishroots.net/FnghTyrn.htm**

Galway

Galway West Family History Society Ltd, Unit 3, Venture Centre, Liosbaun Estate, Tuam Rd, Galway
Tel: (091) 756737, Fax: (091) 753590
Email: **galwayfhswest@eircom.net**
Internet: **www.irishroots.net/WtGalway.htm**
West Galway and Galway city.

East Galway Family History Society Ltd, Woodford Heritage Centre, Woodford, Loughrea, Co. Galway
Tel: (0509) 49309, Fax: (0509) 49546
Internet: **www.irishroots.net/EtGalway.htm**
East Galway only.

Kerry

Killarney Genealogical Centre, Bishop's House, Killarney, Co. Kerry
Tel: (064) 35946
No service (2003).

Kildare

Kildare Heritage & Genealogical Society Co. Ltd, History & Family Research Centre, Riverbank, Main St, Newbridge, Co. Kildare
Tel: (045) 433602, Fax: (045) 431611
Email: **capinfo@iol.ie**
Internet: **www.kildare.ie/genealogy**

Kilkenny

Kilkenny Archaeological Society, Rothe House, Kilkenny
Tel: (056) 22893, Fax: (056) 22893
Internet: **www.kilkennyarchaeologicalsociety.ie**

Laois

Irish Midlands Ancestry, Bury Quay, Tullamore, Co. Offaly
Tel: (0506) 21421, Fax: (0506) 21421
Email: **ohas@iol.ie**
Internet: **www.irishmidlandsancestry.com**

Leitrim

Leitrim Heritage Centre, c/o Leitrim County Library, Ballinamore, Co. Leitrim
Tel: (078) 44012, Fax: (078) 44425

Email: **leitrimgenealogy@eircom.net**

Internet: **www.irishroots.net/Leitrim.htm**

Limerick

Limerick Archives, The Granary, Michael St, Limerick

Tel: (061) 407530, Fax: (061) 312985

Internet: **www.irishroots.net/limerick/index.htm**

Longford

Longford Roots, 1 Church St, Longford

Tel: (043) 41235

Internet: **www.irishroots.net/Longford.htm**

Louth

See Meath

Mayo

Mayo North Family History Research Centre, Enniscoe, Castlehill, Ballina, Co. Mayo

Tel: (096) 31809, Fax: (096) 31885

Internet: **mayo.irishroots.net/Centres.htm**

North Mayo only.

South Mayo Family Research Centre, Main St, Ballinrobe, Co. Mayo

Tel: (092) 41214, Fax: (092) 41214

Internet: **mayo.irishroots.net/Centres.htm**

South Mayo only.

Meath

Meath Heritage Centre, Trim, Co. Meath
Tel: (046) 36633
Internet: **www.iol.ie/~meathhc**

Monaghan

Monaghan Ancestry, Clogher Historical Society, 6 Tully St, Monaghan
Tel: (047) 82304
Internet: **www.irishroots.net/Monaghan.htm**

Offaly

See Laois

Roscommon

Roscommon Heritage and Genealogy Centre, Strokestown, Co. Roscommon
Tel: (078) 33380
Internet: **www.irishroots.net/Roscmmn.htm**

Sligo

Sligo Heritage and Genealogical Centre, Áras Reddan, Temple St, Sligo
Tel: (071) 43728
Internet: **www.irishroots.net/Sligo.htm**

Tipperary

Tipperary Family History Research, The Excel Heritage Centre, Mitchell St, Tipperary
Tel: (062) 80555, Fax: (062) 80552
Internet: **www.tfhr.org**
Catholic registers for Cashel and Emly diocese only.

Tipperary North Family History Foundation,
Governor's House, Kickham St, Nenagh,
Co. Tipperary
Tel: (067) 33850, Fax: (067) 33586
Email: **tippnorthgenealogy@eircom.net**
Internet: **www.irishroots.net/NTipp.htm**
North Tipperary only.

Brú Boru Heritage Centre, Cashel,
Co. Tipperary
Tel: (062) 61122, Fax: (062) 62700
Internet: **www.irishroots.net/STipp.htm**
South Tipperary only.

Tyrone

See Fermanagh

Waterford

Waterford Heritage Ltd, Jenkin's Lane, Waterford
Tel: (051) 876123, Fax: (051) 850645
Email: **mnoc@iol.ie**
Internet: **www.iol.ie/~mnoc**

Westmeath

Dún na Sí Heritage and Genealogical Centre,
Knockdomney, Moate, Co. Westmeath
Tel: (0902) 81183, Fax: (0902) 81661
Internet: **www.irishroots.net/Wstmeath.htm**

Wexford

Wexford Genealogy Centre, Tagoat Community Development, Tagoat, Rosslare, Co. Wexford

Tel: (053) 32610, Fax: (053) 32612

Email: **wexgen@eircom.net**

Internet: **homepage.eircom.net/~yolawexford**

Wicklow

Wicklow Family History Centre, Wicklow's Historic Gaol, Wicklow

Tel: (0404) 20126, Fax: (0404) 61612

Email: **wfh@tinet.ie**

Internet: **www.wicklow.ie/c4_frames/index_heritage.html**

SUPERINTENDENT REGISTRAR'S OFFICES (REPUBLIC OF IRELAND)

Carlow

Community Care Centre, Athy Rd, Carlow
Tel: (0503) 30053

Cavan

Gate Lodge, Lisdarn Hospital, Cavan
Tel: (049) 4371709

Clare

Sandfield Centre, Ennis. Tel: (065) 6868050

Cork (North)

County Council Offices, Annabella, Mallow
Tel: (022) 50230

Cork (South)

Adelaide Court, Adelaide St, Cork
Tel: (021) 4275126

Cork (West)

The Courthouse, Skibbereen. Tel: (028) 23140

Donegal (North)

St Conal's Hospital, Letterkenny. Tel: (074) 23782

Donegal (South)

St Joseph's Hospital, Stranorlar. Tel: (074) 31038

Dublin (City and County)

Ground Floor, Joyce House, 8/11 Lombard St
East, Dublin 2. Tel: (01) 6711968/74

Galway

WHB, 25 Newcastle Rd, Galway
Tel: (091) 523122

Kerry

Registration Office, SHB, Killarney. Tel: (064) 32251

Kildare

EHB, Unit 5, Monread Office Complex, Naas
Tel: (045) 887660

Kilkenny

County Clinic, James Green, Kilkenny
Tel: (056) 52208

Laois

Health Centre, Dublin Rd, Portlaoise
Tel: (0502) 21135

Leitrim

NWHB, Community Care Offices, Leitrim Rd, Carrick-on-Shannon. Tel: (078) 20308

Limerick (City)

St Camillus's Hospital, Limerick. Tel: (061) 326677

Limerick (County)

MWHB, Health Centre, Newcastle West
Tel: (069) 62545

Longford

MHB, County Clinic, Dublin Rd, Longford
Tel: (043) 46211

Louth

Community Care Centre, Dublin Rd, Dundalk
Tel: (042) 9332287

Mayo

WHB, New Antrim St, Castlebar
Tel: (094) 23249

Meath

Town Hall, Trim. Tel: (046) 31512

Monaghan

NEHB, Rooskey, Monaghan. Tel: (047) 30400

Offaly

Health Centre, Arden Rd, Tullamore
Tel: (0506) 41301

Roscommon

WHB, The Courthouse, Roscommon
Tel: (0903) 26518

Sligo

NWHB, Markievicz House, Sligo. Tel: (071) 55115

Tipperary (Northriding)

MWHB, Kenyon St, Nenagh. Tel: (067) 31212

Tipperary (Southriding)

County Clinic, Western Rd, Clonmel
Tel: (052) 77000

Waterford (City)

SHB, Cork Rd, Waterford. Tel: (051) 842824/25

Waterford (County)

St Joseph's Hospital, Dungarvan. Tel: (058) 20900

Westmeath

The County Clinic, Mullingar. Tel: (044) 40221

Wexford

County Clinic, Grogan's Rd, Wexford
Tel: (053) 23522

Wicklow

EHB, Glenside Rd, Wicklow. Tel: (0404) 68400

SUPERINTENDENT REGISTRAR'S OFFICES (NORTHERN IRELAND)

Antrim

Antrim Borough Council, The Steeple,
Antrim BT41 1BJ
Tel: (028) 94481315, Fax: (028) 94464469
Email: **sjm@antrim.gov.uk**

Ballymena Borough Council, Ardeevin,
80 Galgorm Rd, Ballymena BT42 1AB
Tel: (028) 25660352, Fax: (028) 25660400
Email: **personnel.services@ballymena.gov.uk**

Ballymoney Borough Council, Riada House,
14 Charles St, Ballymoney BT53 6DZ
Tel: (028) 27662280, Fax: (028) 27665150
Email: **info@ballymoney.gov.uk**

Carrickfergus Borough Council, Town Hall,
Joymount, Carrickfergus BT38 7DL

Tel: (028) 93351604, Fax: (028) 93366676
Open 9.30–12:30, 2–4 Mon–Fri

Larne Borough Council, Smiley Buildings, Victoria Rd, Larne BT40 IRU
Tel: (028) 28272313, Fax: (028) 28260660
Email: **tennantj@larne.gov.uk**

Moyle District Council, Sheskburn House, 7 Mary St, Ballycastle BT54 6QH
Tel: (028) 20762225, Fax: (028) 20762515
Email: **dev@moyle-council.org.uk**

Newtownabbey District Council, Mossley Mill, Newtownabbey BT35 5QA
Tel: (028) 90340179, Fax: (028) 90340181
Email: **bdm@newtownabbey.gov.uk**

Armagh

Armagh City & District Council, The Palace, Demesne, Armagh BT60 4EL
Tel: (028) 37529615, Fax: (028) 37529617
Email: **info@armagh.gov.uk**

Newry & Mourne District Council, District Council Offices, Town Hall, Bank Parade, Newry BT35 6HR
Tel: (028) 30261512, Fax: (028) 30261416
Email: **administration@newryandmourne.gov.uk**

Belfast

Belfast City Council, City Hall, Belfast BT1 5GS
Tel: (028) 90320202, Fax: (028) 90270520
Email: **registrar@belfastcity.gov.uk**

Castlereagh Borough Council, Civic & Administrative Office, Bradford Ct, Upper Gallwally, Belfast BT8 6RD
Tel: (028) 90494520/1, Fax: (028) 90494525
Email: **gro.nisra@dfpni.gov.uk**

Derry/Londonderry

Coleraine Borough Council, Cloonavin, 66 Portstewart Rd, Coleraine BT52 1EY
Tel: (028) 70347020, Fax: (028) 70347026
Email: **townclerk@colerainebc.gov.uk**

Derry City Council, Guildhall, Londonderry BT48 6DQ
Tel: (028) 71268439, Fax: (028) 71377964
Email: **registrarsoffice@derrycity.gov.uk**

Limavady Borough Council, 7 Connell St, Limavady BT49 0AH
Tel: (028) 77722226, Fax: (028) 77722010
Email: **monica.anderson@limavady.gov.uk**

Magherafelt District Council, 50 Ballyronan Rd, Magherafelt BT45 6EN

Tel: (028) 79397979, Fax: (028) 79300741
Email: **mdc@magherafelt.gov.uk**

Down

Ards Borough Council, Town Hall,
Newtownards BT23 4AP
Tel: (028) 91810803, Fax: (028) 91810803
Email: **heather.canavan@ards-council.gov.uk**

Banbridge District Council, Council Office,
Downshire Rd, Banbridge BT32 3JY
Tel: (028) 40660614, Fax: (028) 40660601
Email: **info@banbridgedc.gov.uk**

Craigavon Borough Council, Civic Centre,
PO Box 66, Lakeview Rd, Craigavon BT64 1AL
Tel: (028) 38312400, Fax: (028) 38312444
Email: **info@craigavon.gov.uk**

Down District Council, 24 Strangford Rd,
Downpatrick BT30 6SR
Tel: (028) 44610825, Fax: (028) 44610801
Email: **kdelaney@downdc.gov.uk**

Lisburn Borough Council, Island Civic Centre,
The Island, Lisburn BT27 4RL
Tel: (028) 92509250, Fax: (028) 92509285
Email: **bdm.registration@lisburn.gov.uk**

North Down Borough Council, Town Hall,
The Castle, Bangor BT20 4BT
Tel: (028) 91278003, Fax: (028) 91271370
Email: **registration@northdown.gov.uk**

Fermanagh

Fermanagh District Council, Town Hall,
Enniskillen BT74 7BA
Tel: (028) 66325050, Fax: (028) 66322024
Open: 9.30–12.30, 2–4.30 Mon–Fri
Email: **fdc@fermanagh.gov.uk**

Tyrone

Dungannon District Council, Council Offices,
Circular Rd, Dungannon BT71 6DT
Tel: (028) 87720329, Fax: (028) 87720333
Email: **contact@dungannon.gov.uk**

Omagh District Council, District Council Offices,
The Grange, Mountjoy Rd,
Omagh BT79 7BL
Tel: (028) 82245321, Fax: (028) 82243888
Email: **amy.smyton@omagh.gov.uk**

Strabane District Council, District Council
Offices, 47 Derry Rd, Strabane BT82 8DY
Tel: (028) 71382204, Fax: (028) 71381348
Email: **admin@strabanedc.com**

FAMILY HISTORY SOCIETIES

Ballinteer Family History Society,
29 The View, Woodpark, Ballinteer,
Dundrum, Dublin 16
Tel: (01) 2988082
Email: **ryan@iol.ie**

Cork Genealogical Society, c/o 22 Elm Drive,
Shamrock Lawn, Douglas, Cork
Internet: **homepage.tinet.ie/~aocoleman**

Genealogical Society of Ireland, 11 Desmond
Avenue, Dún Laoghaire, Co. Dublin
Tel: (01) 2842711, Fax: (01) 2854020
Email: **GenSocIreland@iol.ie**
Internet: **www.dun-laoghaire.com/genealogy**

Irish Family History Society, PO Box 36, Naas,
Co. Kildare
Email: **ifhs@eircom.net**
Internet: **homepage.tinet.ie/~ifhs**

Kerry Genealogical Society, 119/120 Rock St,
Tralee, Co. Kerry

North of Ireland Family History Society,
c/o Graduate School of Education,

The Queen's University, 69 University St,
Belfast BT7 1HL
Email: **webmaster@nifhs.org**
Internet: **www.nifhs.org**

Raheny Heritage Society, 68 Raheny Park,
Raheny, Dublin 5
Tel: (01) 8314729
Email: **jussher@hotmail.com**

The Irish Genealogical Research Society,
18 Stratford Avenue, Rainham, Kent ME8 OEP
Email: **info@igrsoc.org**
Internet: **www.igrsoc.org**

Wexford Family History Society, Carraig Mór,
Maudlintown, Wexford
Tel: (053) 22973

TEN

FURTHER READING

BOOKS

Begley, Donal F. (ed.) *Irish Genealogy: A Record Finder* (Dublin 1981).

Betit, Kyle J. & Radford, D., *A Genealogist's Guide to Discovering Your Irish Ancestors* (Cincinnati 2001).

Evans, M. D. (ed.) *Aspects of Irish Genealogy: Proceedings of the 1st Irish Genealogical Congress* (Dublin 1993).

Evans, M. D. & Ó Dúill E. (eds) *Aspects of Irish Genealogy 2: Proceedings of the 2nd Irish Genealogical Congress* (Dublin 1996).

Gorry, P. & MacConghail M., *Tracing Irish Ancestors* (Glasgow 1997).

Grenham, John, *Tracing Your Irish Ancestors* (2nd ed., Dublin 1999).

Grenham, John, *Clans and Families of Ireland* (Dublin 1993).

Handran, George B., *Townlands in Poor Law Unions: A Reprint of Poor Law Union Pamphlets of the General Registrar's Office* (Salem, Ma 1997).

Mitchell, Brian, *A New Genealogical Atlas of Ireland* (2nd ed., Baltimore 2002).

Mitchell, Brian, *Guide to Irish Parish Registers* (Baltimore 1988).

McCarthy, Tony, *The Irish Roots Guide* (Dublin 1991).

Ryan, Christopher, *Aspects of Irish Genealogy 3: Proceedings of the 3rd Irish Genealogical Congress* (Dublin 1999).

Ryan, James G., *Irish Records: Sources for Family and Local History* (2nd ed., Dublin 1998).

Ryan, James G. (ed.) *Irish Church Records* (2nd ed., Dublin 2000).

JOURNALS

The Irish Genealogist (Journal of the Irish Genealogical Research Society, annual from 1937).

Irish Roots (quarterly since 1992, **www.irishrootsmagazine.com**).

Irish Family History (Journal of the Irish Family History Society, annual from 1985).

North Irish Roots (Journal of the North of Ireland Family History Society, annual from 1984).

Familia — Ulster Genealogical Review (Journal of the Ulster Historical Society, annual from 1985).

Journal of the Genealogical Society of Ireland (quarterly from 2000).